P9-DFQ-962

writers
and their times

Ernest Hemingway
and World War I

Richard Andersen

Cavendish
Square
New York

For Diane and Harvest Love

Published in 2015 by Cavendish Square Publishing, LLC
243 5th Avenue, Suite 136, New York, NY 10016

This publication represents the opinions and views of the author based on his or her personal experience, knowledge, and
research. The information in this book serves as a general guide only. The author and publisher have used their best efforts in
preparing this book and disclaim liability rising directly or indirectly from the use and application of this book.

CPSIA Compliance Information: Batch #WS14CSQ

All websites were available and accurate when this book was sent to press.

Library of Congress Cataloging-in-Publication Data

Andersen, Richard, 1946-
Ernest Hemingway and World War I / Richard Andersen.
pages cm. — (Writers and Their Times)
Includes bibliographical references and index.
ISBN 978-1-62712-809-4 (hardcover) ISBN 978-1-62712-811-7 (ebook)
1. Hemingway, Ernest, 1899-1961—Criticism and interpretation. 2. World War, 1914-1918—Literature and the war. 3.
World War, 1914-1918—Influence. I. Title.
PS3515.E37Z554 2014
813'.52—dc23
2013050653

Editorial Director: Dean Miller	Designer: Amy Greenan
Editor: Kristen Susienka	Production Manager: Jennifer Ryder-Talbot
Senior Copy Editor: Wendy A. Reynolds	Production Editor: David McNamara
Art Director: Jeffrey Talbot	Photo Research by J8 Media

The photographs in this book are used by permission and through the courtesy of: Cover photo by Photo Researchers/Getty Images; Monadori/Getty
Images, 5; Johnny Cyprus/File:Suffragettes demonstrating outside the Police Court.jpg /Wikimedia Commons, 7; Kurt Hutton/
Picture Post/Getty Images, 8; Universal History Archive/Universal Images Group/Getty Images, 10; MPI/Archive Photos/Getty Images, 13;
Ernest Brooks/ File:British wounded Bernafay Wood 19 July 1916.jpg/Wikipedia Commons, 14; AP Photo/National Museum of Health, 16;
ANSA/Universal Images Group/Getty Images, 18; Albert Harlingue/Roger Viollet/Getty Images, 19; Library of Congress/File:Gertrude stein.jpg/
Wikipedia Commons, 20; Margaret C. Anderson/© Yale University Beinecke Rare Book and Manuscript Library, New Haven, CT and The Speiser
and Easterling-Hallman Foundation Collection of Ernest Hemingway, Irvin Department of Rare Books and Special Collections, University of South
Carolina, Columbia, S.C. 29208, 21; Carl van Vechten/File:Francis Scott Fitzgerald 1937 June 4 (2) (photo by Carl van Vechten).jpg/Wikimedia
Commons, 22; JFK-EHEMC/File:ErnestHemingwayBabyPicture.jpg/Wikimedia Commons, 24; JFK-EHEMC /File:Ernest Hemingway with
Family, 1905.png/Wikimedia Commons, 26; George Karger/Time & Life Pictures/Getty Images, 27; Alfred Eisenstaedt/Time & Life Pictures/
Getty Images, 28; Underwood Archives/Archive Photos/Getty Images, 29; Everett Collection Inc./CSU Archive/age fotostock, 30; Fotosearch/
Archive Photos/Getty Images, 32; John F. Kennedy Presidential Library and Museum, Boston/File:Ernest Hadley and Bumby Hemingway.jpg/
Wikimedia Commons, 34; New York Daily News Archive/Getty Images, 37; Acroterion/File:Hemingway House Key West FL1.jpg/Wikimedia
Commons, 38; AP Photo/E. L. Chapin, 39; File:Ernest Hemingway at the Finca Vigia, Cuba 1946 – NARA - 192660.jpg/Wikimedia Commons,
40; © AP, 42; © AP, 43; Herbert Orth/Time & Life Pictures/Getty Images, 44; John F. Kennedy Presidential Library and Museum, Boston/
File:HemingwayLoeb.jpg/Wikimedia Commons, 46; ©akgimages/The Image Works, 47; A. Peda/File:LadyDuffGordon-1917.jpg/Wikipedia, 48;
©akgimages/ The Image Works, 49; Fotosearch/Archive Photos/Getty Images, 51; © AP, 53; Sasha/Hulton Archive/Getty Images, 56; FPG/Archive
Photos/Getty Images, 60; Roger Viollet/Getty Images, 64; Tony Linck/Time & Life Pictures/Getty Images, 66-67; Pictorial Parade/Archive Photos/
Getty Images, 68; Loomis Dean/Time & Life Pictures/Getty Images, 69; Herbert Orth/Time & Life Pictures/Getty Images, 70; Popperfoto/Getty
Images, 73; Apic/Hulton Archive/Getty Images, 75; Topical Press Agency/Hulton Archive/Getty Images, 76; Express/Hulton Archive/Getty Images,
79; © AP, 81; © AP, 82; MPI/Archive Photos/Getty Images, 85; Archive Photos/Moviepix/Getty Images, 88; Anthony Potter Collection/Archive
Photos/Getty Images, 91; Time & Life Pictures/Getty Images, 94.

Printed in the United States of America

writers
and their times

Contents

Illusion and Disillusion

"The world is getting better. The quality of life continues to improve for everyone. The world may never be perfect, but over the course of time, it will get closer and closer." Today, these thoughts are inconceivable. But for almost 400 of the years prior to 1914, they were believed to be true by most Europeans and Euro-Americans.

These ideas were reinforced throughout the late nineteenth and early twentieth centuries by such Industrial Revolution inventions as the railroad, telegraph, camera, telephone, electric light bulb, radio, airplane, automobile, and moving picture, all of which drastically improved many people's quality of life.

What happened in 1914 to change this view of continual progress?

World War I.

Now, scientific knowledge and industrial development were used to destroy life, rather than enrich it. The first weapons of mass destruction appeared during World War I: the machine gun, hand grenade, flamethrower, tank, torpedo, submarine, and mustard gas. When British and French soldiers first experienced German-invented mustard gas, they couldn't see, hear, or feel it. All they knew was that they were literally drowning in their own blood because their lungs had evaporated.

Through the use of advanced weaponry, more people are killed in shorter amounts of time than in any previous time in history. Tens of thousands of sword-wielding Russian cavalry are mowed down by German machine guns in a single afternoon. An estimated 500,000 British, French, and German soldiers die in the Battle of the Marne without having any effect on the outcome of the war. By the time the fighting ends in 1918, more than twenty million people no longer exist.

The war proved that white Europeans and Euro-Americans—at the time, the so-called "most civilized people" in the world—could commit atrocities that were beyond reasonable explanation. Before World War I, life was supposedly like what you read in novels, where you understood the behavior of all the characters.

The bodies of the French soldiers, fallen during a battle with the German army, lying abandoned in the street in Reims, May 1917.

In the wake of the war, literature no longer accurately reflected life, and history no longer told the truth. Even the once popular sentiments of religion and nationalism now came to be seen by many people as evil rather than good. World War I had created a new world. The old one, full of optimistic progress, was history.

A Nation of Change

The world changed after World War I, and many Americans changed with it. Starting in 1915, African Americans took advantage of job opportunities in northern factories, abandoning the South in unprecedented numbers. By bringing with them the art, music, and literature that had rarely been experienced outside of the South, they established cultural centers in the northern cities they migrated to.

Jettisoning the long, heavy, restrictive garments worn before World War I, American women cut their hair short, hiked up their skirts, took jobs outside of the home, and bought their clothes ready-made in stores. They attended college as never before, smoked cigarettes, drank bootleg gin, listened to jazz, rode in automobiles, danced the Charleston, and went to movies. There was more to the women's movement than sexual equality with men.

Fashion, as we understand it today, came into being. Before World War I, people would buy a garment and keep it until they needed a new one. After the war, people were told—and many believed—that they needed new clothes for each new season. The relatively cheap, easy-to-wear, store-bought clothes now available also reflected a growing self-expression by women whose desires and interests no longer conformed to traditional behavior. Their place was no longer necessarily in the home.

What we now call "popular culture" was created, too. Many writers and artists saw the new emphasis on style over substance as crucial to the development of new forms of expression.

Mabel Capper and fellow suffragettes demonstrating outside the Police Court in 1911.

Devotees of serious art, music, and literature, however, saw the popular fascination with money, jazz, fashion, movies, and celebrity gossip as superficial, materialistic, and commercial subjects that should be rejected. Reflection and analysis do not play a significant role in popular culture, and many writers after World War I were highly critical of it.

The Birth of Modernism

Ernest Hemingway was one of these writers. Born in 1899, he grew up under what came to be perceived as the illusions of the past. He suffered physical and mental trauma brought on by his experience in World War I, and wrestled with the disillusionment that followed. Along with many other writers, he searched for new meaning and values in the world created by the war, and new ways of representing that world through his poems, short stories, and novels.

Pajama-clad author Hemingway writes up copy for a report on World War II in Europe. Hemingway was a war reporter and correspondent for the United States Ist Army.

There's a name for this search for new meaning and its representation—"**Modernism**." Modernist painting, sculpture, music, dance, architecture, and literature rejects many of the ways these art forms represented life before World War I as being false, unreliable, arbitrary, or artificial. To a Modernist, art can only reflect fragments of who we think we are—or want to appear as—to others. To the post-war Modernist, poems were little more than artificial constructs that didn't reflect the way people actually spoke. Dance forms, such as ballet, rigidly precluded the natural way people moved to music. And music that always sounded pleasant to the ear, regardless of its subject matter, did not accurately echo the harsh, discordant noise of life.

If you've ever attended a modern dance performance, listened to jazz, marveled at the height of a skyscraper, observed a painting and couldn't make out what the artist claims is being depicted, or read a book where the beginning, middle, and end didn't appear in chronological order, you've experienced Modernism.

British soldiers line the trenches during World War I.

ONE

The Great War and the Lost Generation

World War I—often called the "Great War"—which raged from July 1914 to November 1918, was the greatest catastrophe ever experienced by humankind up to that time. Referred to as the "war to end all wars" by U.S. president Woodrow Wilson, it was fought on two fronts: the eastern front pitted mostly Russians against Germans, and the bitterly fought western front, which pitted mostly British and French forces against Germans and introduced the strategy of **trench warfare**. These trenches, which ran almost uninterrupted from Belgium to Switzerland, shattered whatever idealism many of the soldiers had when they signed up to fight. People no longer fell to the ground and died as they had in past wars; now they were blown through the air, exploded into pieces, or literally drowned by mustard gas.

Ten million soldiers on both sides died in combat, an unprecedented number that was attained by technological advancements, the slaughter of massive waves of attacking humans, and the resulting entrenchment of armies waiting for a battle strategy that could outdo this improved weaponry. Because antibiotics did not yet exist, two million more soldiers died of disease. Seven million civilians also perished during the war, and another six million civilians as well as soldiers were never heard from again.

The Horrors of War

Before World War I, war was seen as a romantic adventure. People who returned home from battle had been celebrated in parades as heroes. The dead were honored in memorials with their names carved on them. In 1854, Alfred Lord Tennyson wrote a poem commemorating a British cavalry charge against Cossack forces in the Crimean War. It was called "The Charge of the Light Brigade." Part of it read,

> When can their glory fade?
> O the wild charge they made!
> All the world wonder'd.
> Honor the charge they made!
> Honor the Light Brigade,
> Noble six hundred!

Wilfred Owen, who was born in 1893 and died in battle one week before World War I ended in 1918, wrote about combat from the soldiers' point of view. In his most famous poem, "Dulce et Decorum Est," Owen uses the **dehumanization** of war to undermine the idealism of British schoolboys who, as he once did, studied combat from the viewpoint of poets like Tennyson. His honest descriptions of soldiers at war, however, saved neither him nor those who have followed him since.

> Bent double, like old beggars under sacks,
> Knock-kneed, coughing like hags, we cursed through sludge,
> Till on the haunting flares we turned our backs

"Uncle Sam" recruitment poster.

And towards our distant rest began to trudge.
Men marched asleep. Many had lost their boots
But limped on, blood-shot. All went lame; all blind;
Drunk with fatigue; deaf even to the hoots
Of tired, outstripped Five-Nines[1] that dropped behind.

Balance of Power

What's ironic and tragic about World War I is that it was
unnecessary. For the hundred years preceding the Great War,
Europe was a relatively peaceful place. Playing a large role in

---

1 Five-Nines are the mortar shells that landed in the trenches that the
soldiers had just left.

British and German walking wounded on the way to a dressing station near Bernafay Wood, July 1916.

maintaining that peace was a system of protective alliances. No country could attack another without having to also fight the countries it was aligned with. Unfortunately, that didn't stop Austria-Hungary from declaring war on Serbia after a Serbian **nationalist** assassinated Archduke Franz Ferdinand, the next in line to sit on the Austrian-Hungarian throne. Nor did it stop Serbia's ally, Russia, from declaring war on Austria-Hungary. Because Austria-Hungary was aligned with Germany, Germany then declared war on Russia. France, because of its alliance with Russia, declared war on Germany. When Germany marched through Belgium to attack France, Great Britain, which was aligned with Belgium, also declared war against Germany.

Other countries rushed to join the slaughter: Turkey joined up with Central Powers Germany and Austria-Hungary, while Italy and Japan threw in their lot with the opposing Allies, France and Great Britain. By 1915, the combined armies numbered more than seventy million soldiers, most of whom had dug themselves into opposing trenches that no side could attack without being cut down by rapid-firing machine guns.

Before the first year of fighting had drawn to a close, opposing armies on the western front found themselves entrenched in a virtual stalemate. Then, in the summer of 1916, the Allies took the offensive. The Battle of the Somme opened with the bloodiest day in history. More than 19,000 soldiers died. By the time it was over, the British army suffered 420,000 casualties, the French 200,000, and the Germans 500,000—all without having any effect on the outcome of the war. When the Allies finally did achieve victory in 1918, they'd lost the lives of ten million soldiers and recovered only eight miles of the territory originally seized by the invading Central Powers.

Death didn't end with the fighting. Disease proved even worse than bullets. Somewhere between fifty and one hundred million people throughout the world died from influenza, or flu, when infected soldiers returned home.

America Enters the War

Watching the massacre from across the Atlantic Ocean—and growing increasingly rich by supplying munitions to any country with the money to pay for them—was the United States. American bankers lent money to those countries that couldn't afford to pay outright, and by 1916, some of the larger banks were in danger of going out of business from huge unpaid war loans. Unwilling to let the banks go under, the once neutral American government prepared to enter the conflict on the side of its greatest debtor, Great Britain. To do this, it had to convince the American people that entering Europe's killing trenches was a moral obligation. It wasn't hard, and it didn't take long. When the country learned it was Germany that had invented the dreaded machine gun, flamethrower, and mustard gas, and it was German-invented submarines that had begun

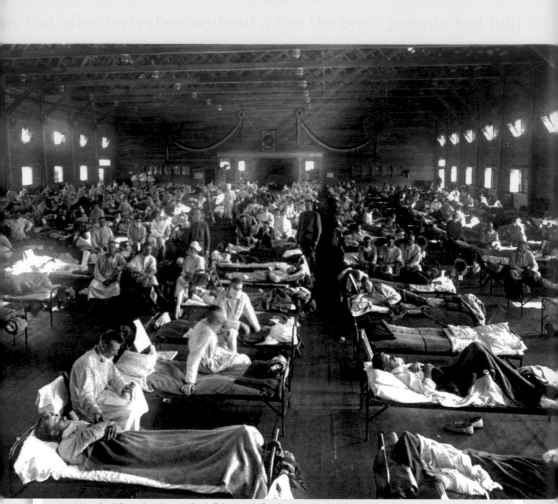
Many buildings became makeshift hospitals for those wounded during the war.

The Spanish Flu

The Spanish flu epidemic is said to have run from January of 1918 to December of 1920. Nobody knows exactly when it began, but the first to be severely impacted were German and Austrian soldiers during World War I. Some historians say it may have even tipped the balance of war in favor of the Allies.

When the flu first started to infect large numbers of soldiers on both sides of the conflict, the warring countries tried to downplay its significance, fearing troop morale would suffer.

Soldiers with Spanish flu weren't sent home but to hospitals where the disease spread even more quickly.

The first Spanish flu outbreak in the United States occurred when a cook at Fort Riley, Kansas reported feeling sick on March 4, 1918. By March 11, one hundred more soldiers had come down with the flu. A few days later, that number rose to five hundred. Not only did the disease spread quickly, it traveled as far as remote islands in the Pacific and areas in the Arctic.

We know today, thanks to samples frozen during the epidemic, that it was not the flu that actually killed its victims. The healthiest immune systems overreacted to the virus, killing the person as well as the disease. Most post-war Spanish flu-related deaths were otherwise healthy people under the age of sixty-five.

The Spanish flu stopped just as suddenly as it appeared. No one knows exactly why. It keeps coming back, however. Today it's known as H1N1.

torpedoing defenseless ships carrying innocent Americans across the Atlantic, the American people quickly rallied around President Wilson's call to make "the world safe for democracy." Congress declared war against the Central Powers on April 6, 1917, and the United States, with its vast supply of raw materials, arms, and people, assured victory for the Allies. Nevertheless, by the time the fighting ended, 250,000 American soldiers were dead.

Expatriate Communities

Americans fighting in World War I were exposed to more than bullets and the Spanish flu, however. While in cities such as London, Milan, and Paris, tens of thousands of American soldiers found their own country to be culturally lacking, intellectually narrow, spiritually shallow, obsessively materialistic, and depressingly reactionary by comparison. Thanks to the **Eighteenth Amendment**, you couldn't legally drink a glass of wine in your home unless you made it in the basement. Nor within a few years could you read James Joyce's *Ulysses* or

The *Lusitania* sinking forward, eighteen minutes before exploding in 1915.

American Bar on the Avenue des Champs-Élysées in Paris.

watch a dancer perform if her name happened to be Josephine Baker. Many repatriated soldiers, as well as individuals who hadn't fought in the war but felt intellectually and emotionally constrained by the conservative climate sweeping America in reaction to it, made their way back across the Atlantic. No place served as a greater magnet for them than Paris.

Paris in the 1920s

With its tree-lined boulevards, ornate architecture, numerous cafés, incomparable cuisine, and favorable exchange rate, as well as the free-spirited tolerance of its people, the City of Light provided an attractive setting for Americans looking to fill the void created at home by the rising tide of conservative restrictions. Many of these "reverse immigrants" squandered their talent having a good time, their creativity limited to mastering the self-absorbed sensibilities and superficial manners of café culture. They knew something was missing in their lives but

Gertrude Stein coined the term "Lost Generation."

were too busy eating, drinking, and enjoying life to do much about it. Some thought socializing on this level was what life was all about. The American expatriate and writer Gertrude Stein, who had been living in Paris since 1903, had a word for these often opinionated, frequently **nihilistic**, terminally bored loafers. She called them the "Lost Generation."

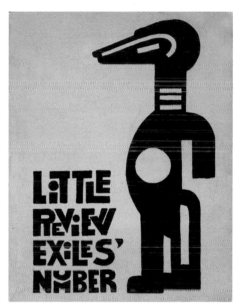

A copy of *The Little Review*, spring 1923.

The Lost Generation

"Lost Generation" is a catchall phrase for the disillusioned living in Paris and other European and American capitals during and after World War I. However, many of the writers, artists, and musicians of the time did not consider themselves lost. A sense of ruin may have swept across the once belligerent nations, but their new expressions of that ruin were almost always original.

Unfortunately for these and other writers, not many readers were interested in their new forms of expression. Most preferred mysteries, westerns, and romances as an escape from their own harsh post-war reality. While many Modernist writers of the Lost Generation, like Ezra Pound, may have dreamed of celebrity and financial success, they had to settle for seeing their works printed in "little magazines." *The Little Review*, *transatlantic review*, and *This Quarter*—the three that have become legendary—were called "little" because they had few pages, a small audience, limited budgets, and only paid

F. Scott Fitzgerald, circa 1937.

Americans in Paris

Paris after World War I was considered the cultural capital of the world. Many American writers and artists chose to live on the Left Bank, where they established several English-language bookstores and English-language magazines.

their writers a dollar a page, most of which they got back when the writers whose works they published purchased copies of the issues in which their works appeared. At the same time, their editors didn't concern themselves with advertisers, stockholders, or subscribers. This allowed them to focus on what they wanted to print, not what they felt they had to print to make a profit. By the time the magazines folded, they'd published close to eighty percent of all the important new writers in the years following World War I. Of these writers, only Ernest Hemingway would join F. Scott Fitzgerald in the land of fame and fortune.

The most famous of all these bookstores was the American Sylvia Beach's Shakespeare & Company, which became a social center for this tightly knit community of expatriates. Hemingway met Ezra Pound there. He introduced Ernest to Gertrude Stein. She introduced him to just about everybody else she thought he should know, including T.S. Eliot, Archibald MacLeish, John Dos Passos, Edmund Wilson, e.e. cummings, Gerald and Sara Murphy, Djuna Barnes, and F. Scott Fitzgerald.

Fitzgerald was a celebrity when he arrived in Paris in April 1925. He'd already published *This Side of Paradise* (1920), *The Beautiful and the Damned* (1922), and *The Great Gatsby* (1925). Fitzgerald was instantly rich, delicately handsome, slight of frame, undisciplined in his work, unable to control the alcohol he consumed, and codependent on his unstable wife, Zelda. Hemingway was ruggedly handsome, powerfully built, maintained a strict writing schedule, was proud of his ability to hold his liquor, and had to work as a journalist and rely on his wife Hadley's trust fund to make ends meet. Fitzgerald couldn't have been more unlike Hemingway, yet the two became friends.

Ernest Hemingway as a baby, circa 1900.

TWO

The Life of Ernest Hemingway

Ernest Miller Hemingway was born on July 21, 1899 in Oak Park, Illinois. Ernest hated both his given names for being what today we might call wimpy. His friends called him "Hem."

Ernest's mother, Grace, was a serious musician who left her parents' home in Oak Park at twenty-two to become an opera singer in New York. Following her Madison Square Garden debut in 1895, she returned in 1896 to marry the young, conservative, God-fearing doctor across the street. A suffragette who insisted on naming each of her six children and designing the family home, Mrs. Hemingway required her husband to do all the shopping and cooking so she could focus on the music lessons that brought in more money than his obstetrics practice. When Ed Hemingway put a pistol to his head in 1928, Ernest placed more of the blame on his mom's "selfish independence" than his father's advanced diabetes and disastrous real estate investments.

Ernest was also angry with his father for taking away the special relationship they shared. Dr. Hemingway had taught him to hunt, fish, swim, and hike. An expert angler by the time he was five, Ernest spent his first seventeen summers at the family cottage on Walloon Lake in northern Michigan.

Early picture of Ernest Hemingway with his family. From left: Marcelline, Sunny, C. E. Hemingway, Grace Hemingway, Ursula, and Ernest standing at the far right, 1905.

Family Life and School

Ernest developed a love of writing by keeping a diary and sending letters from Walloon Lake to friends and family in Oak Park. A standout in English, he often displayed mature sensitivity to literature. His teachers showered him with praise, and he rewarded them with thought-provoking essays, parodies of poems, a column in the school newspaper, and stories in the school's literary magazine.

Ernest was brawn as well as brain. But at six feet and only 150 pounds, he lacked both strength and coordination.

Hemingway gave boxing lessons to Ezra Pound, F. Scott Fitzgerald, and Harold Loeb, the model for Cohen in *The Sun Also Rises*.

Constantly berated for not pulling his weight on the high school football team, he pleaded with his reluctant father to pay for boxing lessons. During the first lesson, Ernest's coach asked him if he'd like to go a few rounds with the gym's highest-ranking middleweight. Ernest went down with a broken nose before he had a chance to throw a single punch. Nevertheless, he showed up the next day, ready for whatever the coach was prepared to throw at him.

This story serves as a metaphor for an issue that Hemingway wrestled with all his life: what it means to be a man. In this regard, there were two Hemingways. There was the Ernest who sang in the church choir, played the cello, took dance lessons, joined the debate club, got good grades, and was named Class Prophet. And then there was the Ernest who, at the age of two, insisted he was "'fraid a nothin.'" These three words started out as a family joke but were repeated so often Ernest felt he had to live up to them if he wanted to be respected as a real man. All his life he would try either to prove his bravery or prevent others from thinking him cowardly.

Like many children, Ernest made up stories in which he starred as the hero, but as he grew older, he tried to live them. He imagined himself as a combination of the "grace under fire" type found in the works of Rudyard Kipling and the outgoing, masculinist hero of a Ring Lardner short story. He even created a name for this private side of himself: Hemingstein.

Newsroom at the *Kansas City Star.*

Kansas City Star

It was the underdeveloped Hemingstein who resisted his family's pressure to attend college. He wanted to be where men were measured by the kind of action not found in the protective environment of a school—in short, the real world.

The real world rejected Ernest for poor eyesight when he tried twelve times to enlist in the army after America entered World War I in April of 1917. Fortunately, his uncle Tyler found him what might have been the next best thing: a reporter job with the *Kansas City Star.* This was the kind of action with heroes and villains that Ernest had only read about. Now he was up close and personal with all kinds of unsavory characters.

Equally important was the newspaper's celebrated style. Write short sentences. Use vigorous words. Focus on the action. From his first day on the job in October 1917 to his last in April 1918, Ernest transformed these principles into a style he would become closely identified with. But he always added something to his short stories and novels that wasn't in the paper's principles of good writing. He always sought to include a comment on the larger human condition through the action he described.

Ernest quickly became friends with another reporter at the *Star*. Ted Brumback had recently returned from driving an ambulance in France and was eager to get back to a level of excitement not possible in Kansas. By May 1918, Hemingway and Brumback were parading with 75,000 other Red Cross volunteers through Madison Square in New York. Two months later, on July 8, the newly commissioned second lieutenant was lucky to be alive. Ernest had been handing out chocolate and cigarettes to Italian troops when a shell exploded within three feet of him. It immediately took the life of a man standing nearby, tore the limbs from a number of other men while the cigarettes still hung from their lips, and deposited more than two hundred pieces of **shrapnel** in Ernest's legs. Despite his serious wounds, Ernest threw one of the injured soldiers across his back and carried him to a first aid station. He was just nineteen years old.

Red Cross nurses greeting our boys at the pier in New York City, December 30, 1918.

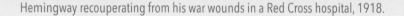

Hemingway recouperating from his war wounds in a Red Cross hospital, 1918.

American Volunteers and the Red Cross

Long before the United States declared war on Germany in April of 1917, large numbers of Americans volunteered to aid the Allied cause. Canada, as part of the British Empire, had been fighting the Central Powers since the war began in 1914, and many young American men joined the Canadian armed forces, including the writer William Faulkner. By 1916, American pilots had organized their own combat force: the famous Lafayette Escadrille. Named after the French aristocrat who supported the American Revolution against England in the eighteenth century, the squadron became an attack wing of the French flying forces, saw significant front-line action, and suffered heavy casualties as a result.

At the same time, 300,000 men and women across the country volunteered for service in the American Red Cross between 1914 and 1917 and helped to set up aid stations, outfit hospitals for war wounds, and organize effective ambulance squads all along the western front and into northern Italy.

While the Red Cross was heavily endorsed and funded by the United States government, many private citizens also supported the organization's work. Within one stunning week in May 1917, Americans contributed more than $115 million to aid the effort to save lives.

On July 17, Ernest was transported from the front lines to a convalescent hospital in Milan. There he met the only woman in his life to have had more influence over him than his mother: Agnes von Kurowsky. An American Red Cross volunteer, Agnes was lively, vivacious, and considerably more worldly than the handful of young men in her care, all of whom fell in love with her. Although he was six years her junior, it was the handsome, intelligent, shy-in-a-masculine-kind-of-way Ernest who caught her eye. The two fell in love, and Agnes switched to the night shift to spend every night with him. Ten years later, she would become the model for Catherine in the novel that would solidify Hemingway's reputation as one of the great writers of his generation: *A Farewell to Arms* (1929).

First Love

Agnes was transferred to Florence in October 1918, and Ernest, with the help of a cane, headed back to the United States three months later. Their plan was for him to get a job and for them to join hands in matrimony. Ernest had never been so happy. Not only was he enjoying the first great romance of his life, he found himself being celebrated as a war hero. Sporting two ribbons of valor on the Spagnolini-designed uniform he'd had made in Milan, he paraded about Oak Park in an Italian officer's cape and knee-length cordovan boots. Speaking at schools and civic functions, he showed off the guns he brought home from the front but had never fired, used his cane for longer than necessary, and held before his audiences the blood-soaked pants he was wearing when he nearly lost his leg.

Ernest also began telling the same kinds of stories he used to make up as a child with himself as hero. There was some truth to each of the stories, but the elaborations were often difficult to believe, despite being told in Hemingway's famous understated style. There is no doubt Ernest was sprayed with shrapnel, but did an Italian machine-gunner accidently lodge

Nurse Agnes von Kurowsky, Ernest Hemingway, and two other American Red Cross nurses at the San Siro horse racing track in Milan, Italy, circa 1918.

two bullets in his leg? Hemingway's hospital report doesn't mention this. And did he really toss his two Italian medals for bravery into the bowl holding the 227 pieces of shrapnel next to his hospital bed? It's almost as if carrying a wounded soldier to safety wasn't heroic enough.

Rejection

Then came the "Dear John" letter that began, "Dear Hem." Agnes broke Ernest's heart when she wrote to him of her engagement to an Italian army officer who was to inherit a dukedom. Later, when the officer's family objected on the grounds that she was not of their class, she confided her pain to Ernest, who was not consoled. Giving vent to his feelings in the appropriately entitled, "A Very Short Story" (1924), Ernest licked his romantic wounds, but he never got over them. They would appear in different forms—not only in his behavior, but also in much of what he wrote.

Heartbroken, Ernest spent the summer of 1920 physically and emotionally limping around the Walloon Lake family cottage. He couldn't sleep at night, and nothing he wrote was bought by any magazine. His parents treated him as the boy he'd been when he left home, instead of the war hero he had now become. This led to a series of disagreements that Ernest would later relive in his short story, "A Soldier's Home" (1925). They also motivated him to move to Toronto and later Chicago, instead of returning to Oak Park with his family in the fall. It was in Chicago that he met the pretty, shy, and eager-to-please Hadley Richardson.

Eight years Ernest's senior, the combination of Hadley's trust fund and recent inheritance could modestly support them both, and by January 1922, they were married and living on the same street as Ezra Pound in Paris. Gertrude Stein was also in the neighborhood. It wasn't long before the Hemingways began rubbing elbows with the international colony of Modernists that had flocked to the city after World War I: James Joyce, Pablo Picasso, and Sylvia Beach. Several years later, the newly arrived F. Scott and Zelda Fitzgerald would also become friends with the young couple who rivaled them in looks, if not in fame.

While a lot of time was spent in cafés, Ernest didn't follow the usual pattern of meeting in the afternoon and drinking late into the night. He started his day in the isolated Closerie des Lilas with coffee, paper, and two new pencils. Not until he tired

Hadley Richardson

From left: Hadley, John (Bumby), and Ernest Hemingway.

Red-headed, blue-eyed Elizabeth Hadley Richardson was born into money and privilege on November 9, 1891. During her sheltered St. Louis girlhood, she attended the Mary Institute, an exclusive school founded by T.S. Eliot's grandfather. Like Ernest's mother, Hadley was an accomplished musician. Shy almost to the point of being withdrawn, however, she gave up a promising career as a concert pianist when she was just eighteen.

John Dos Passos wrote that Hemingway always left his wives "more able to cope with life than he found them." This was certainly true of Hadley. Under Ernest's tutelage, she grew from what her mother described as an "invalid who shouldn't even spend a night alone" to an independent, self-confident woman who went on to marry Paul Scott Mowrer, the first foreign correspondent to receive a Pulitzer Prize. Her son with Ernest grew up to father two other famous Hemingways of his own: Margaux, a model, and the actress Mariel.

of writing would he head for one of the cafés where writers, artists, and intellectuals frequently met.

Because drinking every night in cafés, eating regularly in restaurants, skiing in Switzerland, sunbathing on the Riviera, and following bullfights in Spain strained Hadley's trust fund, Ernest became a foreign correspondent for the *Toronto Daily Star*. The work also helped Ernest rediscover his own writing voice. He stopped trying to produce the slick commercial fiction found in popular magazines and concentrated instead on the sparse, unadorned sentences that characterized his work as a journalist. These stories appeared in several literary magazines in Paris and were eventually collected in the United States for Ernest's first major publication: *In Our Time* (1925).

All was not well with the Hemingways, however, and the birth of a son in 1923 failed to shore up the cracks that had begun to appear in their marriage more than a year earlier. As Hadley grew increasingly focused on caring for the baby they nicknamed Bumby, Ernest found in his wife's best friend the continued adoration he apparently couldn't do without. Pauline Pfeiffer was intelligent, witty, and slim-figured, with unlimited financial resources and a distinct sense of fashion that included a boyish haircut and a coat made of chipmunk. By comparison, she made Hadley seem dull and dowdy.

Love and Fame

Only four years older than Ernest, as compared with Agnes's six and Hadley's eight, Pauline won the handsome writer over with her unwavering support for everything he said and did. He began secretly sharing with her the final drafts of what would be his first novel, *The Sun Also Rises* (1926), and within a year of its publication, he'd divorced Hadley to marry her. He'd also started working on the first book to make enough money to enable him to write without having to work for someone else: *A Farewell to Arms* (1929). *Scribner's Magazine* paid a record $16,000 for the serial rights and the book became a runaway best seller, despite being released a month before the start of the Great Depression in 1929.

Ernest was now more than a writer struggling to get his work accepted. He was a celebrity. The fame lasted—but not his marriage to Pauline. Nevertheless, the twelve years they lived, loved, and fought at their homes in Florida and Wyoming were the most productive of Ernest's career, spanning the publication of his World War I novel, *A Farewell to Arms* (1929), to the release of his novel about the Spanish Civil War, *For Whom the Bell Tolls* (1940).

When not writing, Ernest spent his time perusing his libraries of more than 7,000 books, hunting in Wyoming in the summer, fishing off the coasts of Florida and Cuba in the winter, drinking at a run-down bar in Key West known as Sloppy Joe's, and having affairs with numerous women, including Martha Gellhorn. Only twenty-eight, she was already an established journalist. Ambitious, talented, and spirited like Agnes von Kurowsky, but not as willing to serve and please as Hadley and Pauline, Martha inspired Ernest to return to Europe in 1937 to cover the Spanish Civil War, and then write about it in *For Whom the Bell Tolls*. Nominated for the Pulitzer Prize, the novel sold half a million copies within months of its release.

Martha encouraged Ernest to report on the Second World War as early as 1939, but he chose instead to search the Caribbean for German submarines in his battle-readied fishing boat. He did, however, return to Europe in time for the Allied invasion in 1944. Although he fabricated stories about being a part of the landing in France, he did accompany the 22nd Infantry in Normandy, left it temporarily to lead a small band of partisans, and was amongst the first to help liberate Paris. He did not, as he later boasted, liberate the Ritz Hotel. In 1947, America awarded Ernest the Bronze Star for bravery.

Pauline Pfeiffer and Ernest Hemingway, 1934.

Hemingway's famous house at Key West.

Somehow in his action-packed life, Ernest was able to
find time to divorce Pauline in 1940 and marry Martha two
weeks later in Wyoming. They rarely got along very well, and
Hemingway's responses were almost always vindictive. When
he replaced Martha as *Collier's* war correspondent in Europe
during World War II, he was able to prevent her from acquiring
the press credentials that would allow her to fly to London.

Martha Gellhorn, 1941.

She was forced to sail on a ship laden with explosives. By the time she arrived, he'd been in an automobile accident, fallen in love with *Time* correspondent Mary Walsh, and asked her to marry him. Martha was not sympathetic, and during their divorce in Havana in 1945, he took advantage of the Cuban law that entitled him to keep all of his former wife's possessions. Mary became Ernest's fourth wife—and she might not have been his last if she hadn't outlived him.

Man of Action

By this time in Hemingway's life, two patterns emerge. The first pattern concerns the courage upon which his legend as a hero rests. Although there is no question of his bravery, British Air Marshall Peter Wykeham, who flew Ernest in a hopeless pursuit of German V-1 rockets toward the end of World War II, did note in the *London Times*, "He impressed me as the sort of man who spends his whole life proving he is not afraid." Others, too, have suggested an unhealthy connection between Ernest's image of himself and his behavior. They claim he is not so much a man of action as a man acting out his own insecurities.

The second pattern involves Ernest's last three marriages. After the first to Hadley Richardson, Ernest's relationships with Pauline Pfeiffer, Martha Gellhorn, and Mary Walsh all began as secret affairs while he was still married. He would hold on to each wife until his relationship with the next woman was

Hemingway at his Cuban villa Finca Vigia in 1946.

secure. Then he'd go through a painful separation and divorce. Could he have been protecting himself by leaving his wives before they could leave him, as Agnes von Kurowsky had done? Ernest also found in each new wife, as well as in many of the women with whom he had affairs, something of a muse. He often said his best writing was done when he was in love. F. Scott Fitzgerald went so far as to claim, "Ernest needs a woman for each new book." The many loves he won and lost appear mostly in two forms—submissive or aggressive— throughout many of his short stories and novels.

Hemingway may have written a number of books while in the throes of love, but his talent didn't keep pace. Rarely in the almost two dozen years following the publication of *A Farewell to Arms* in 1929 did his writing rise above the level of good reportage. But when an expanded chapter from a novel he was working on came out in 1952, it restored Ernest's tarnished reputation. Titled *The Old Man and the Sea*, it was in an issue of *Life* magazine that sold five million copies in two days, won the Pulitzer Prize, and played an important role in his winning the Nobel Prize for Literature in 1954. Except for *A Moveable Feast* (1964), a collection of sketches he'd written about some of the people he knew while living in Paris in the twenties and published after he died, that was the extent of his best work.

There was a lot of pain in Ernest's life, emotional as well as physical. Tall, big, and athletic-looking, if somewhat clumsy, he was plagued with illnesses and physical injuries all his life. The most severe came from two plane crashes in two successive days while in Africa on a safari—another of his many attempts to demonstrate his courage, this time by taking down big game animals with high-powered rifles.

Drinking proved to be an effective antidote for a lot of these hardships, but it adversely affected his behavior as he got older. The somewhat shy, endearingly masculine boy in his twenties became a truth-stretching braggart in his thirties, a heartless

Hemingway and his wife Mary Welsh at home, 1960.

bully in his forties, a drunken boor in his fifties, and a delusional paranoid by the time he turned sixty. Just before he died, the electric shock treatment he received for depression and frequent mood swings robbed him of his short-term memory and his ability to write so much as a single sentence. It was possibly the worst fate of all for a writer who put words on paper nearly every day of his life.

Ernest woke early on the morning of July 2, 1961 in his cabin in Ketchum, Idaho. Mary was asleep upstairs. He had a job to do, and he went about it with the same "grace under pressure" he was noted for all his life. Slipping two shells into a shotgun, he pressed the butt end against the floor and the double-barreled end just above his eyebrows. He then tripped both triggers, and was gone forever.

THREE

The Sun Also Rises

The Sun Also Rises (1926) is considered one of Ernest Hemingway's best novels. One of the reasons why may be the speed with which he wrote it. He began the book on his twenty-sixth birthday in 1925 and finished a first draft four months later. Previously, everything he wrote had taken a lot of time and energy. Rarely would he go on to the next sentence of any story until the one he was working on was as close to perfect as he could get it. Then, he would begin his next writing day by re-reading everything he'd written from the very first word. He always found something to change; something could always be improved upon.

With *The Sun Also Rises*, however, Ernest wrote so quickly he often had a hard time keeping up with the words as they raced through his mind. Capturing the immediacy of feeling for a series of events he'd often experienced only a few weeks earlier seemed almost effortless. Of course, Ernest devoted a lot of time to revisiting and rewriting once his first draft had been completed, but the difference between the way this story was

Ernest Hemingway seated in 1925 with the persons depicted in the novel *The Sun Also Rises*. (From left:) Hemingway, Harold Loeb, Lady Duff Twysden, Hadley Richardson, Ogden Stewart, and Pat Guthrie.

written and his approach to previous stories was that he hadn't tried to write and edit at the same time. He wrote down all that came into his mind about a particular person or event, and then, afterwards, he edited the seven notebooks he'd compiled. This enabled him to forge the unadorned prose for which he is known without losing the conversational tone of voice he captured in the first draft.

The experience that grabbed Ernest's imagination—and revolutionized his writing process—was a tour of bullfights he and Hadley had organized with several of their café-hopping friends from Paris. These included the free-spirited, frequently inebriated, promiscuous Lady Duff Twysden, to whom Ernest was physically attracted, and Harold Loeb, a Princeton-educated writer and enthusiastic supporter of Ernest's writing. To say the trip was a disaster is an understatement. Nevertheless, the competiveness, jealousies, and hostilities it generated among the members of the party inspired Ernest to write at a level he was rarely again able to attain. Lady Duff proved proud to have served as the closely rendered model for Brett Ashley, and the devoted Loeb saw as a betrayal Ernest's choice to represent him as the unappealing Robert Cohn. Until he came up with the name of Jake Barnes, Ernest referred to the novel's first-person narrator as "Hem."

Hemingway sitting in front of a sick steer during one of his bullfighting trips to Pamplona, Spain, 1927.

Lady Duff: The Original Lady Brett

Lady Duff Twysden was thirty-two years old when she traveled to Spain to attend the San Fermin Feria bullfights in 1925. Married to naval officer Sir Roger Twysden since 1917, the two had become bitterly separated. Short of money, she was often in the company of Patrick Gutherie, an alcoholic Scotsman who supported Duff's decadent lifestyle at the humiliating expense of his own. With her bobbed hair, slim figure, fondness for alcohol, and promiscuous nature, Duff was often a focus of attention for many of the men in her life. When Ernest found out Duff and Harold Loeb had enjoyed a weeklong secret liaison in St. Jean-de-Luz in France, he became jealous, and the barely disguised arguments that erupted between them almost came to blows. Ernest got the last word, however, when he portrayed Loeb as the unattractive Cohn in *The Sun Also Rises*. While Duff wasn't spared either, she did not mind serving as the model for Lady Brett Ashley. Her only recorded response was to point out that she hadn't slept with a bullfighter, as Brett had done in the novel.

Ernest had been regularly attending bullfights in Spain since the summer of 1923. He loved participating in the amateur events that preceded them, including using a jacket or sweater to challenge a yearling bull whose horns had been padded. Running ahead of the bulls stampeding through the streets of Pamplona during the San Fermin **Fiesta** in 1924, he caught the attention of the press and turned what was a relatively unknown annual ritual into an international event. Photos of the American **aficionado** Ernest Hemingway hobnobbing with **matadors** soon became part of every excursion. One of them, Niño de la Palma, would later play a crucial role in *The Sun Also Rises* as the inspiration for Pedro Romero.

Ernest wanted his café friends in Paris to see for themselves what a hero he was, and a good number went along for the thrill. No group created quite the stir, however, as those who attended the bullfighting pilgrimage of 1925: Lady Duff (whom a besotted Ernest later claimed to have no respect for), Hadley (whose radiant smile appeared only when Niño de la Palma awarded her the severed ears of a bull), and

Hemingway (in the white hat) with Pauline Pfeiffer (to his left) attending a bullfight.

Harold Loeb (whose romantic appeal to Lady Duff and distaste for the cruelty inherent in the sport almost brought him to blows with Ernest), all brought out the worst in each other. That Ernest could create understanding and even sympathy in his story for these mostly unattractive people is a true measure of his ability. He skillfully allowed his readers' emotions to build while conveying in simple sentences the unadorned facts of their behavior. Ernest captured the nihilism and aimlessness of post-World War I life in *The Sun Also Rises* so well, and in such an appealing way, that the critic Malcolm Crowley observed young women modeling themselves after Lady Brett and young Midwestern men trying to look, talk, and act like Hemingway heroes.

Plot Synopsis

The Sun Also Rises opens with its narrator, an American journalist named Jake Barnes, telling us about his friend Robert Cohn. A World War I veteran, Jake doesn't have much respect for anyone who hasn't been in combat. We are told that while the wealthy Cohn did not serve in the war, he was a boxing champion at Princeton and is now a successful writer living in Paris. Cohn, complaining about his controlling girlfriend, asks Jake to come with him to South America. Jake refuses, reminding Cohn he'll be the same person in South America that he is in Paris.

That night, Jake runs into Lady Brett Ashley, a selfish, free-spirited, twice-divorced Englishwoman. Although the two are in love, a war wound has rendered Jake sexually impotent, leaving Brett unwilling to commit to him. At the same time, she can't find happiness with any other man. For most of the time they're together, Brett confides in the forlorn Jake about her love affairs and trysts.

When Cohn later tells Jake of his attraction to Brett, Jake informs him of her engagement to Scottish veteran

Poster advertising the 1924 San Fermin Festival.

Mike Campbell. That same afternoon, Jake is supposed to meet Brett at a café, but she stands him up. Instead, she comes to his apartment that evening with a wealthy Greek, Count Mippipopolous. Mippipopolous loves Brett but won't make a fool of himself for her, as almost every other man in the novel seems destined to. When Mippipopolous leaves to buy champagne, Brett tells Jake she is leaving for a vacation in Spain, explaining it will be easier on her if they are apart for a while.

Several weeks pass. Jake and a war buddy, Bill Gorton, arrange a fishing trip to Spain, where they will later attend the bullfighting fiesta in Pamplona. Hearing of this, Cohn makes plans to join them. Jake runs into Brett and her fiancé, Mike, who then plan to join the party at the bullfights. When Mike is out of earshot, Brett tells Jake that she and Cohn had a brief affair during her vacation in Spain.

Jake, Bill, and Cohn travel to Pamplona. Brett and Mike delay their arrival with a side trip to San Sebastian—the same place Brett went with Cohn several weeks earlier. Jake and Bill decide to go fishing as they planned, while Cohn pines in Pamplona for Brett.

Jake and Bill, who make the happiest twosome in the novel, have a fine time fishing and enjoying the Spanish countryside. When Mike lets them know in a letter that he and Brett will be leaving San Sebastian, Jake and Bill head for Pamplona, where they stay in a hotel run by a bullfighting aficionado named Montoya. Montoya likes Jake because, unlike most foreigners, he understands what bullfighting is all about. When Jake, Bill, Cohn, Mike, and Brett finally get together, Mike—drunk as usual—attacks Cohn for following him and Brett around.

When the fiesta begins, so do the fireworks. Nineteen-year-old matador Pedro Romero sets himself apart from all the other matadors by the beautifully executed risks he takes in his ritualized combat with the bulls. Brett can't take her eyes off him and, a few days later, asks Jake to introduce her to the

Actress Ava Gardner is flanked by co-stars Mel Ferrer, left, and Tyrone Power, right, during the filming of a bullfight scene for the motion picture *The Sun Also Rises* in Mexico City,1957.

handsome angel of death. Jake agrees to help the woman he loves meet with Romero.

While Brett trysts with Romero, Jake meets Mike and Bill at a café, where they have been drinking. Cohn shows up in search of Brett. Unable to contain himself, Mike insults Cohn. Jake, drowning his frustrations in drink, joins in. Cohn winds up punching them both out before continuing his search for Brett. When Jake returns to the hotel, he finds Cohn crying on his bed. He's ashamed for having clobbered Jake and asks his forgiveness. Reluctantly, Jake shakes Cohn's hand and the blow is forgiven, if not forgotten. The next day, he learns that Cohn also attacked Romero when he discovered him with Brett. No matter how many times Cohn knocked Romero down, the matador kept trying to get up. Later, when Cohn asks for his forgiveness, Romero refuses.

The following day, the swollen and bloodied Romero brilliantly fights and kills a bull and bestows upon Brett the creature's ear. The two take off for Madrid shortly afterwards. The next morning, Mike, Bill, and Jake discover that Cohn has left for Paris. They, too, go their separate ways, with Jake deciding to unwind in San Sebastian. He's not there long, however, when he receives a telegram from Brett. She's out of money and wants him to meet her in Madrid.

When Jake arrives, Brett tells him she broke off her relationship with Romero because she felt she would damage his career. When she tells him she wants to return to Mike, Jake sympathetically books two tickets to Paris. As they ride in a taxi toward the Madrid train station, Brett tells Jake that they could have had a wonderful time together, to which Jake replies, "Yes, isn't it pretty to think so?"

Cultural Context

The cultural context of this story can be summed up in the novel's epigram: "You are all a lost generation." Pronounced by Gertrude Stein, the expression soon made its way through Hemingway into the popular culture. The term "Lost Generation" refers to the many millions of people suffering from the shock of World War I, their subsequent disillusionment with the values of the past, and their inability to find relevant meaning in the new, indifferent, seemingly purposeless world created by the war. The lost characters we meet in *The Sun Also Rises* spend most of their time drinking in cafés, conversing superficially with other seemingly rudderless people, and engaging in casual affairs for lack of anything better to do.

No one in the novel seems more lost—or more at a loss regarding what to do with her life—than Lady Brett Ashley. No matter how much she drinks, how many lovers she takes, how often she travels, or how much money men may spend on her, significant mental and emotional fulfillment constantly elude her. Her one selfless act is ending her relationship with Pedro Romero, the young, idealistic bullfighter, because she fears she will corrupt him.

In contrast, Robert Cohn still believes in the kind of love he's read about in novels and sees no reason why he can't be Brett's knight in shining armor. He doesn't realize that these ideals are no longer viable because the world no longer believes in ideals. He runs away with Brett for a romantic holiday—never sensing that, for her, their time in Spain is only an escape from the frustration of not being able to consummate her relationship with Jake. Cohn later makes a nuisance of himself with Brett and her fiancé Mike Campbell, not realizing his presence is no longer appreciated. He makes everything worse by beating up Romero upon discovery of the matador's affair with Brett. Embarrassed by his self-abasing behavior, Cohn sneaks away from the party in Pamplona without saying goodbye to anyone. Brett, meanwhile, will surely continue beyond the pages of the novel to drink, dance, and otherwise engage in the kinds of **escapist** behavior that can only leave her unsatisfied, unfulfilled, and unhappy.

1920s flappers imitating the "Brett Ashley look" made famous in *The Sun Also Rises*.

Stein's quotation about the Lost Generation is not Hemingway's only epigram, however. Through a long passage from Ecclesiastes, he tells us that no matter what might happen in our short lives, the Earth will continue; the sun will also rise. While it is true that a new generation will dawn as surely as the sun, the action of the novel does not offer much to look forward to. History has proven the novel, if not Hemingway, right.

Major Characters

Jake Barnes

Jake Barnes and Ernest Hemingway have a lot in common. Veterans of World War I, they've been wounded physically and emotionally by their experiences in combat. They live in Paris, work as journalists, drink heavily, enjoy fishing, have trouble sleeping at night, are passionate about bullfighting, prefer the company of men who've proved themselves in combat, and love women who cared for them while they were in hospitals recovering.

Jake, like Hemingway, while a member of the Lost Generation—suffering many of the same anxieties and frustrations as his contemporaries, wandering from café to café—is not lost. Rather, he's on a quest to discover how to live in a world that has reduced the human condition to little more than meaningless activity. The journey is not a smooth one. He wallows in self-pity, treats others cruelly, and follows Brett around like a lost puppy, even to the point of facilitating her relationship with Pedro Romero. But he also learns from the courageous, uncompromising, self-possessed Romero the importance of never giving up and always maintaining dignity. Cohn knocks the matador down fifteen times, but he can't knock him out. Romero keeps trying to rise to his feet, keeps throwing punches, and when Cohn tires of clobbering him, refuses to shake hands. The trained boxer has every advantage over the matador except one: he doesn't have the self-respect that Hemingway admires, Jake lacks, and no fist can touch. The first sign that Jake is beginning to understand and act in accordance with the code by which Romero lives becomes apparent in the final lines of the novel. When Brett laments how they could have had such a good time together, Jake replies, "Isn't it pretty to think so?" Though sadder, he is also wiser. He now knows his manhood depends not on his ability as a lover, but having the courage and self-control to maintain his dignity in a world shattered by war, disillusionment, and the absence of any significant meaning.

Brett Ashley

Brett is the most contemporary character in *The Sun Also Rises*. Independent of mind and spirit, she cuts her hair short, drinks heavily, and enjoys the company of whomever she wants. Men find her irresistible—in Pamplona, they dance around her as if she's some kind of goddess. But she's not happy. Wandering from relationship to relationship almost as aimlessly as she goes from café to café, Brett pines for her true love, Jake Barnes, who can't reciprocate her affection because of the war wound that has rendered him impotent.

Life hasn't been kind to Brett. Her first love died during the war. She then married the alcoholic Lord Ashley, who made her sleep on the floor while he slept with a gun. She met and fell in love with Jake while serving as his nurse. They once tried to make a go of it, but it didn't work out. Engaged to the alcoholic Mike Campbell, who's in line for a huge inheritance, she still seeks fulfillment in the arms of Cohn, albeit briefly. Her engagement also doesn't stop Brett from pursuing the dashing, handsome Pedro Romero, whom Cohn clobbers upon discovering their affair. The very next day, the matador gives Brett the ear from a bull he's killed and they're off to Madrid. The jealous Cohn, ashamed of his behavior, skips town.

What's the thirty-four-year-old adolescent to do? For the first time in the novel, and perhaps the only time in her life, Brett decides to act like an adult. Knowing what a corrupting influence she might be on the matador fifteen years her junior, she breaks off their relationship. Another experiment in escapist love having ended in an empty hotel room, Brett then summons the ever-reliable Jake, a constant reminder of the happiness she might have found had the war not intervened. But Jake no longer shares this singular view. He's finally accepted the fact that it is not only his wound that has prevented their union. Brett is incapable of mature love, preferring brief flings to a committed relationship. The book ends with these two characters, each impotent in their own way and for different reasons, thinking about how pretty it otherwise might have been.

Robert Cohn

Robert Cohn is Princeton University's former middleweight boxing champion and a recently published novelist. A Jew and the only non-veteran among the men on their way to Pamplona, he is also an outsider.

Cohn falls in love with Brett at first sight, believing in the romances he's read about in novels but about which his life experience has taught him little. He doesn't see Brett's using him as an escape from her frustrating relationship with Jake. He can't accept Brett's rejection when she is in the company of her fiancé, Mike Campbell. He also can't stop making a fool of himself—he not only decks Jake and Mike outside a café in Pamplona, he also repeatedly pounds Pedro Romero upon discovering him with Brett. It's not until the matador refuses to accept his apology that Cohn understands the degree to which he has humiliated himself.

In many ways, Cohn isn't much different from the other men in the novel who fall in love with Brett, suffer rejection

The running of the bulls in Pamplona, Spain, 1930.

because they can't satisfy her, try to drown their pain in drink, and don't know when to quit trying to be the only man who can rescue her from herself. The difference, of course, is that Cohn didn't fight in the war. Jake and Mike, both veterans, feel they have some kind of unspoken license to treat Cohn in ways they wouldn't think of treating each other or their other male companion in Pamplona, the American vet Bill Gorton. Cohn suffered anti-Semitic abuse at Princeton—he's used to that—but because he can't understand the comradeship that comes from having experienced combat, and because his infatuation with Brett is unrealistic, he loses control of his emotions and physically subdues those he can't conquer any other way. Having won a few battles but lost the war for Brett, Cohn sneaks out of Pamplona under the cloud of his own shameful behavior.

Pedro Romero

Pedro Romero is the ideal man, at least in Hemingway's eyes. Young, handsome, brave, incorruptible, dignified, self-controlled, and highly skilled in the field that gives meaning to his life, Romero's only flaw is a bull-bestowed scar on his cheekbone. Worn as a medal of honor, the scar is still the matador's only flaw when the novel ends.

Embodying many of the qualities that Cohn lacks and Jake desires, Romero exposes their fawning dependence on Brett and their inability to form a code of conduct for themselves that doesn't drip with irony or self-pity. When Cohn savagely beats him, the nineteen-year-old bullfighter refuses to lapse into unconsciousness. Even when he can no longer get to his feet, he keeps swinging at Cohn from his position on the floor and tells the former college boxing champion he will kill him if he isn't out of town by morning.

The next day in the bullring, still suffering from the bruises inflicted on him by Cohn, Romero conducts a clinic in self-possessed heroism. Not only doesn't he favor his wounds, he refuses to take advantage of a bull with defective vision. On the contrary, he puts himself in greater danger by playing to the bull's strength, thus bringing out the best in the animal as well as himself. It's an incredible performance, and he does it not to please Brett—he never even looks up at her from the bullring—but to perform his art at a standard he can be proud of. This nobility may very well have been a consideration in her decision to break up with the matador: she has too much respect for him to risk corrupting him as she has so many others.

Pedro Romero ends his role in the novel with his dignity intact—a triumph not lost on Jake Barnes. With Romero as a model and his neurotic attachment to Brett slipping behind him, Jake now has the opportunity to realize his strengths and regain the integrity he lost in the emotional fallout of World War I.

Major Themes

The Lost Generation

Because the war was unnecessary, it created a crisis of confidence in the institutions that had made millions of casualties possible: government, business, the Church, even family. Where were people to look for guidance in how to live a meaningful life when all the institutions that defined what was meaningful had proved themselves false? Some turned to religion for an answer. Others began searching for a new set of values to replace the ones that had been lost during the war.

Then there were those who didn't even bother to believe or search. The war had taught them there was no higher meaning in life, and integrity, honesty, decency, and trust were only words. The best anyone could hope for was to have a good time. These people became the Lost Generation.

Brett Ashley, Mike Campbell, and many of the characters in *The Sun Also Rises* give life to the phrase, "Lost Generation."

Because they believe existence is meaningless, they live meaningless existences. They wander aimlessly from café to café, party to party, and country to country engaging in inconsequential activities that amount to little more than the passage of time.

Hemingway, on the other hand, was not lost. His ambition was to write, to be an important literary chronicler of the people and events of the time in which he lived. He may have gone to a café every day, but it was an isolated place where he could create without distractions. And what he wrote is critical of "lost" characters like Brett and Mike. He is also critical of Robert Cohn for trying to hold on to values that no longer apply. Bill Gorton and Pedro Romero are the types Hemingway admires. He admires Jake, too, to a lesser extent. Despite the damage inflicted by the war and Brett, by the novel's end, Jake is already putting the unfulfilled life of drink and debauchery behind him, while looking forward to creating a code of behavior more in line with what he experienced in the company of Gorton and Romero.

The Heroic Code

Among the traditional values that were lost during World War I was the idea of what it means to be a man. Before the war, men were supposed to be brave, stoic, honorable, selfless, and dependable. But by the war's end, these words had become meaningless. People don't kill up close and personal like they used to—now, machines do the job. Survival, not conquest, is what counts.

The war veterans in *The Sun Also Rises* are not traditional warrior types. They've been reduced to less than real men, as symbolized by Jake's **impotence**. When they gang up on Cohn for the "unmanly" way he follows Brett, their behavior reveals their own masculine insecurities.

The character that best personifies the heroic code Hemingway admires is Pedro Romero. Romero faces death every time he enters the bullring. But he doesn't flinch, he doesn't cheat, and he doesn't compromise his integrity. When he fights a bull

American music hall star Josephine Baker (1906–1975), pretending to play the clarinet at the Caf' Conc festival at the Stade Buffalo velodrome, Montrouge, Paris, 1926.

with poor eyesight, he uses his skill so as not to take advantage of it. He also applies the same values outside of the ring. When Cohn knocks him down repeatedly, he struggles to his feet and refuses to give up. When Brett tells him she wants to terminate their affair, he accepts what she says and doesn't follow her around, as Cohn did. He doesn't drown his sorrows in alcohol like Mike Campbell. And, ultimately, he doesn't abase himself as Jake did when he facilitated their relationship.

Hemingway knows that courage is not a constant. A person who behaves bravely one day may not do so the next. To address this, he creates a code for Pedro Romero to rely on to maintain his self-control. It enables him to consistently act with "grace under pressure." What's ironic about this expression is that it comes from one of Hemingway's earliest influences on what constitutes manly behavior: Rudyard Kipling. Instead of creating a new definition of masculinity for the levels of awareness created by World War I, Hemingway turned to a code of behavior that he learned before he entered high school. In this sense, he is very much like Cohn—stubbornly holding onto and trying to live by values that are no longer viable. That Hemingway fell short of this heroic ideal in his personal life is one measurement of how difficult it is to maintain this concept outside of a novel. To his credit, he died trying.

Major Symbol

Bullfighting

For Hemingway, bullfighting is a complex ritual with many layers of meaning. He sees it, first of all, as a life and death struggle, even though the outcome is always the same. The fact that the bull always dies is irrelevant; what's important is the symbolic significance of the combat between animal and matador. It serves as a reminder that death eventually comes to all of us; it cannot be put off indefinitely, no matter how valiant the fight.

Bullfight spectators share in the life and death struggle between the bull and the matador the same way fans watching other athletic events vicariously experience the triumphs and defeats of their sports heroes. The difference is that in the bullring, winning and losing is not determined by a score; it always ends in death. Those who feel deeply the life and death struggle that takes place in the arena, and respect, honor, and fear the bull as well as admire, honor, and identify with the matador, are aficionados. Hemingway, a true aficionado, understands and expresses what the athletic contest/dance with death is all about.

Bullfighting is also an art form where one's success depends not so much on killing the bull—anyone with a big enough weapon can do that—but the way the killing is done. It has to follow a certain ritual. Specific movements, almost as in a choreographed dance, have to be followed, and these movements have to be done with skill, courage, self-control, and dignity. The matadors who possess these skills are heroes. Those who don't are just fancy-dressed butchers.

Pedro Romero possesses all the virtues of a true matador. These virtues are not limited to the bullring, however. They are evident in his everyday behavior. To internalize these virtues as a code by which one lives one's life is nothing short

Spanish matador Luis Miguel Dominguin (1926–1995) down on one knee during a bullfight, Pamplona, Spain, 1947. He was the subject of Ernest Hemingway's book *The Dangerous Summer*.

Hemingway with actor Gary Cooper and friends at the Stork Club in New York City, 1943.

of creating meaning in a world where there isn't supposed to be any. In essence, it is to be heroic. This is what Jake Barnes learns from his pilgrimage to Pamplona. He accepts his war-torn fate, but he will no longer let it get the better of him. He accepts the reality of his relationship with Brett, but he is no longer willing to abase himself for her pleasure.

Hemingway, who had little patience for those who wasted their lives drinking, dancing, and debauching their way to death, also wanted to number among those who live by the heroic code. He was close in his youth and during the war, but the very same temptations that in his eyes doomed the Lost Generation distracted him in later years: sex, money, and celebrity.

Hemingway as a celebrity on the cover of *Life* magazine, 1960.

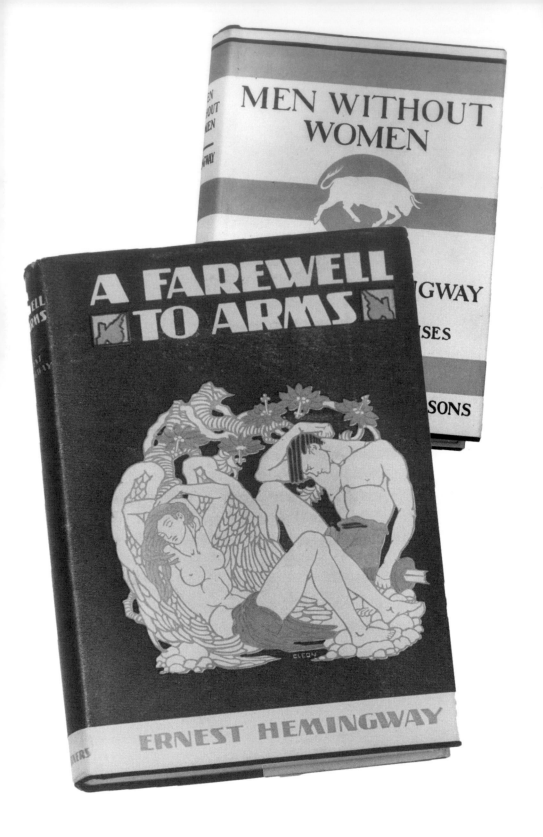

FOUR

A Farewell To Arms

While enjoying the critical and somewhat popular success of *The Sun Also Rises*, Hemingway went back to writing short stories. It was common at the time for writers to publish short stories, come out with a collection, and then follow the collection with a novel. A collection of short stories, *In Our Time* (1925), preceded *The Sun Also Rises* (1926), and another collection, *Men Without Women* (1927), would precede *A Farewell to Arms* (1929).

A Farewell to Arms started out as a short story, partly because it was common practice and partly because short stories were all Hemingway had time for. However, his feelings about the war and his relationship with American Red Cross volunteer Agnes von Kurowsky inspired a longer, deeper exploration, with which he quickly became obsessed.

This proved to be a good thing: given the trauma that accompanied the writing, he might not have otherwise been able to get much work done. First, there was the pressure of the fourteen-month, not-so-secret affair with Pauline Pfeiffer he'd been carrying on since 1925. Then, there was the birth of John—called "Bumby"—from his marriage to Hadley, their separation in 1926, and the subsequent divorce settlement, in which Ernest willingly turned over to them all the rights to *The Sun Also Rises*. His marriage to Pauline followed in 1927, and within a year, the couple moved in with Pauline's family in Arkansas so she could give birth to their first son in the United States. Patrick was born in Kansas City on June 28, and just before the end of the year, Ernest's father killed himself.

A Farewell to Arms was written in Paris, France; Piggott, Arkansas; Kansas City, Missouri; Sheridan, Wyoming—where Ernest fled with his fishing rod to escape the domestic complications of wife, newborn, and in-laws—and Oak Park, Illinois, where Dr. Hemingway had died. There was also a stay in Key West, Florida before returning to Paris, where Ernest wrote seventeen endings before settling on the final version. He wasn't thirty years old, and one month after the book came out in 1929, the stock market crashed.

Almost as impressive as the writing is the research Hemingway conducted. No longer could detractors say he merely fictionalized his experiences. All the facts in his novel are exactly as history has recorded them. He'd been following the war closely since the day he was introduced to wire service at the *Kansas City Star* in 1917. When he returned to Oak Park after being wounded in Italy in 1919, he read everything about the war that he could get his hands on. The battle lines are where Ernest says they are, the troop movements are exactly as he describes, and events, such as the killing of Italian officers during the retreat from Caporetto, really did happen where he says they did. Even the rain that falls in the novel is historically accurate.

Then there was Ernest's personal experience, not only in the front lines at Fossalta di Piave but also in his work as a reporter for the *Toronto Star* after he and Hadley moved to Paris in 1921.

Hemingway pictured with his catch while on a fishing trip, circa 1944.

His first big assignment was to cover the retreat of the Greek army and the hundreds of thousands of refugees who followed from Thrace during the Greco-Turkish War in 1922. The many specific details he recorded could only have come from an eyewitness, and the ones he recreated in *A Farewell to Arms* could only have been described by a writer considerably more talented than most newspaper reporters. Hemingway's depiction of the retreat from Caporetto constitutes one of the most sustained narratives in the novel.

A Farewell to Arms is more than just an accurate war story, however. It's a love story as well. Recuperating from the shrapnel his leg took on the night of July 18, 1918, Ernest became infatuated with an American nurse caring for him at the Red Cross Hospital in Milan. Agnes von Kurowsky was pretty, bright, witty, energetic, fluent in French and German, and six years older than her patient. Surviving a mortar attack, carrying a wounded soldier to safety, and enduring the pain of having more than two hundred pieces of shrapnel removed from his leg gave Hemingway the courage to vie for her affections. Agnes found Ernest's still-innocent vulnerability very appealing, and they soon fell in love.

But the romance was not to last. After Ernest returned to the States in January of 1919 to find a job and plan a wedding, Agnes fell in love with an Italian officer who would someday be a duke. Ernest, who'd been addressed in letters as the light of Agnes's existence, her dearest and best, her "Ernest of Ernests," a hero, and a god, was devastated, angry, and felt betrayed and abandoned. Nevertheless, his romantic feelings would never run as deep, and he chose to recapture them in his portrayal of Catherine Barkley in *A Farewell to Arms*. At the same time, he may have chosen to vicariously revenge Agnes's rejection by killing off Catherine at the end of the novel.

Completed ten years after the love and war experiences that inspired it, *A Farewell to Arms* won almost universal praise from

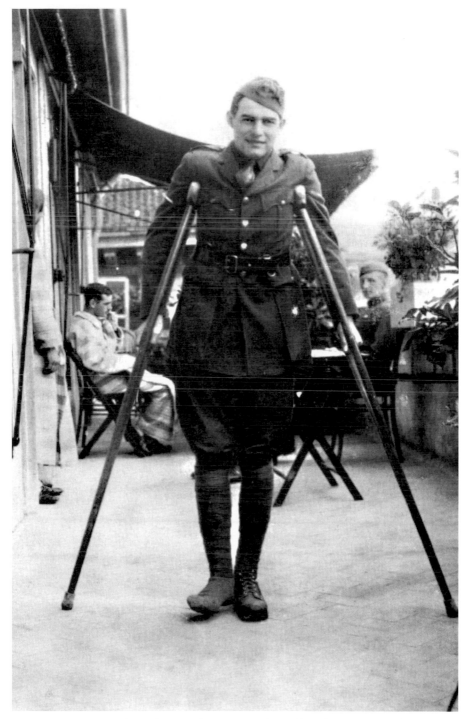

Ernest Hemingway, during his convalescence in Milan, Italy, at the American Red Cross Hospital in 1918.

Italian alpinists defending an attack from a trench dug into the mountain during the First World War.

critics, sold more than 80,000 copies in its first year (despite
the Great Depression), and 1,800,000 by the time Hemingway
died in 1961. It's still in print.

Plot Synopsis

Lieutenant Frederic Henry is an American ambulance driver
in the Italian army during World War I. While waiting for
the orders that will bring him to the front lines, he befriends a
kind, sensitive, idealistic priest from Abruzzi whom the soldiers
taunt for his chaste lifestyle. Conversely, Frederic also befriends
the earthy, warmhearted, frequently drunk, and promiscuous
surgeon, Dr. Rinaldi, who introduces him to Nurse Catherine
Barkley. Frederic and Catherine engage in a flirtatious relationship before Frederic is shipped out to the front. He thinks she's
a little crazy.

When Frederic almost loses his leg to shrapnel, he is transferred to a hospital in Milan where Catherine nurses him back
to health. The two genuinely fall in love, and once Frederic is
able to walk with crutches, they go to the races, ride about in
open carriages, and drink lots of wine. Catherine soon discovers
she is going to have a baby and worries that it will be a burden
to Frederic. Frederic is not pleased with the news, but quickly
adjusts to the idea of a child in their lives. When he is ordered
back to the front, the lovers pledge themselves to each other.

The Italians preparing for battle are tired of war and debate
what would happen if they just stopped fighting. While some
want to continue for honor and glory, the priest from Abruzzi
confesses he doesn't care who wins. The men no longer have the
energy to tease him, and Rinaldi is concerned that he might
have syphilis. Frederic tries not to think of Catherine.

When the Austrians break through the Italian lines, retreating
soldiers and massive numbers of refugees clog the roads, pre-
venting Frederic and his team of ambulance drivers from getting
to where they are most needed. Trying an alternative secondary

Reportage or Literature?

Ernest Hemingway is one of the world's best-known writers. He's also a limited one. He raised newspaper reporting to the level of art, but he lacked the imagination to turn his novels into great literature. He could record, but he couldn't create.

Few more literary writers could capture as vividly Pedro Romero's battle against the bull with the deficient eye in *The Sun Also Rises* or the Italian retreat from Caporetto in *A Farewell to Arms*. However, many less talented writers could make us feel more intensely the psychological battles raging in the minds of the novels' main characters. Jake Barnes doesn't tell us in *The Sun Also Rises* how he feels when he learns Brett has run off to Spain with Robert Cohn, and we don't know how he feels about introducing Brett to Pedro Romero and enabling their romance. Why? Hemingway couldn't capture on paper the emotional traumas taking place inside Jake's head. All he could do was describe a scene and record the action.

We are shocked when Frederic Henry shoots the sergeant who refuses to obey his order in *A Farewell to Arms*—nothing the officer has said or done can explain this extreme action. We conclude as readers this is what war does to people, but we don't have a clue about the internal process that allowed it to happen to Frederic. When his child is stillborn and Catherine dies shortly afterward, Frederic expresses no emotion for the dead baby, compares Catherine's dead body to a statue, and leaves it up to us to imagine how we would feel if we were in his place. Tapping into our already-held emotions for a given situation instead of creating emotional responses stemming from characters we've come to know and care about, however, has more to do with style than substance. It's the same style that characterizes the slick, commercial fiction of which Hemingway was so contemptuous.

Hemingway (center, right, with moustache) in a trench with fellow war correspondents during the Spanish Civil War, circa 1937.

Style is big for Hemingway, both in literature and in life. Small words and short sentences create the impression of realism and objectivity. When combined with terse exchanges of dialogue, his texts carry remarkable suggestive power. And nowhere does Hemingway's talent as a reporter come closest to art than in *The Sun Also Rises*, when he creates a plot that is as seemingly aimless as the characters who inhabit it. It's a genuine ***tour de force*** of which any writer could be proud. But when we analyze the individual characters in both these novels, there's not much substance to them. The women are either aggressively selfish like Brett Ashley, or submissively codependent like Catherine Barkley. The men come in three forms: unemotional heroes like Pedro Romero, wimps like Robert Cohn, and pitiable souls like Jake Barnes and Frederic Henry. We know a lot about what they do, but not much about who they are.

The same can be said of Hemingway. From the time he announced at the age of two that he was "fraid a nothin," he began searching for a style that would match his image of who he was. He created stories with himself as the hero, and then became a hero during World War I. The tailor-made uniform, knee-length boots, officer's cape, and medals for valor enhanced his self-image but also created a model of behavior that was difficult to live up to. Often, he did–he single-handedly saved a boat full of reporters from capsizing during the Spanish Civil War, and he was awarded the American Bronze Star for the risks he took to write eyewitness accounts of the action in France during World War II. But it wasn't enough. For most of his life, he would place himself in dangerous situations, come out alive, and then speak about his participation in these events as if he was still a child telling stories with himself as the hero.

What he did seem to be afraid of was women, especially strong-willed, independent, and spirited types such as his mother, Agnes von Kurowsky, and Martha Gelhorn. But even as supportive a wife as Pauline Pfeiffer could make Ernest cower occasionally. At her suggestion, he included a church scene in *The Sun Also Rises* as well as in *A Farewell to Arms*, and had Frederic of the latter novel pray to God while Catherine lay dying. To please her, Ernest also converted to Catholicism, and claimed he'd been baptized into the Catholic Church by a hospital chaplain. He also refused to acknowledge the authenticity of his marriage to Hadley because they hadn't been wedded by a priest, thus allowing him and the rigidly religious Pauline to be married at a nuptial mass.

Hemingway didn't write about himself as a thinly disguised hero or romantic adventurer, however, and this is where his genius is most intriguing. The central figures in his early novels–Jake Barnes and Frederic Henry–may be closer to the Hemingway that existed behind the heroic persona: whiners and losers who feel they don't deserve what happened to them. They drape themselves in a kind of worldly toughness, but it doesn't protect them where they are most vulnerable: in their hearts. Hemingway's own war with the self-perceived coward he didn't want anyone to discover left him disillusioned, depressed, and drifting from one desperate encounter with love and death after another. Nevertheless, he had the courage to keep going, to remain true to his vision, even to take his own life rather than allow it to be taken from him. He might not have been much of a role model, yet he often exhibited the heroic qualities he esteemed throughout his life.

Colonel Edgar E. Glenn, left, presented the Bronze Star Medal for meritorious service during World War II to Hemingway at the U.S. Embassy at Havana on June 13, 1947.

Army recruits who answered the call to war fill a street in New York, April 1917, shortly after President Woodrow Wilson declared war on Germany.

road, one of the trucks gets bogged down in mud. He then shoots an engineer who refuses to help free the truck.

The whole country now seems to be in chaos. Officers are being executed on the spot for deserting their troops. Fearing he might be mistaken for an Austrian because of his American accent, Frederic dives into a nearby river, floats downstream, and hops a freight train for Milan. He reunites with Catherine in Stresa, and the two soon make their way to neutral Switzerland.

Frederic and Catherine spend the winter in an idyllic mountain cabin. The air is clean, Frederic grows a beard, and the war seems far away, though he sometimes feels guilty for having deserted his army comrades. In the spring, they move to Lausanne to be near a hospital where Catherine can give birth. The boy is stillborn, however, and Catherine hemorrhages to death later than night.

Frederic is numb. He seems not to care about the dead boy, and doesn't say goodbye to Catherine. He walks back to their hotel in the rain. Having bid farewell to the arms of war, he is now left without the arms of his beloved.

Cultural Context

The cultural context of *A Farewell to Arms* can be summed up in one word: War. When war is declared, the news is often met with excitement and anticipation. Horace's old lie—"It is sweet and fitting to die for one's country"—is still believed, especially by the innocent, romantic children who will be doing the fighting. Hemingway was no exception. When the United States entered World War I in April of 1917, the eighteen-year-old was among the first to try to enlist. He saw it as a great adventure. Had he not been rejected for poor eyesight, he might very well not have lived long enough to write the war stories that made him famous. Ernest was that naïve and, at the same time, determined to prove himself brave.

Hemingway never relinquished his idea of the glory and honor to be found in staring death in the face and courageously accomplishing what had to be done to temporarily postpone his own mortality. However, he also observed and recorded the horrendous effects war had on the ordinary men and women trying just to stay alive. Nowhere is this more apparent in *A Farewell to Arms* than in the disastrous retreat after the Italian defeat at Caporetto. What's especially powerful about Hemingway's description of this event is how closely he sticks to the action, allowing the reader to imagine for himself the effect modern-day combat is having on the soldiers. When Frederic shoots an engineering sergeant for refusing to help free an ambulance that's stuck in mud, there is never any indication from Hemingway as to whether he thinks this lieutenant's behavior is right or wrong. Instead, he shows us how totally amoral war is. Shooting a man for refusing an order isn't much different than pushing a truck out of the mud—an analogy that is underscored when no one objects to Frederic's wounding the sergeant, or when one of the soldiers in Frederic's command puts the engineer out of his misery with a bullet to his head. There's no glory here, or even any meaning beyond the literal level of the action: A gun is fired. A man is dead. End of story.

Frederic finds himself in a similar position as he stands in a line of officers who are accused of having deserted their troops. There is no proof, because none is needed. The man in front of Frederic is so shocked by what's happening he can't think of a word to say in his own defense. Fearing his American accent might cause him to be mistaken for an enemy spy, Frederic decides to live rather than die ignobly for something he hasn't done and a cause he never believed in. He runs from the line and jumps in a river, symbolically washing away any sense of duty he may have had to the military. Through this act, he is reborn with a renewed sense of what is most important in his life: Catherine and the love they share.

A recruitment poster from 1918 shows a sailor holding a depth charge full of TNT.

The war will not leave the lovers alone, however. The "separate peace" Frederic has found turns out to be little more than wishful thinking, and his romantic idyll with Catherine in neutral Switzerland is short-lived. Their baby is born dead, and Catherine dies several hours later. It is not just war that is relentlessly meaningless. Love, life, war, and death are all the same in the end: nothing more than a series of losses with only temporary relief. The novel concludes with no catharsis, no epiphany, no revelation, and no affirmation of any kind.

Major Characters

Frederic Henry

The name "Frederic Henry" has a softer, somewhat more effeminate sound than the shorter, harsher-sounding names of some of Hemingway's other heroes, like Jake Barnes of *The Sun Also Rises*. Hemingway hated the name "Ernest" for the same reason.

But Frederic, despite the removal of the masculinist "k," is no softy. He sees war for the evil it is, and words such as "honor" and "glory" are meaningless to him. A soldier with a wound identical to the one Hemingway suffered in 1918, Frederic has learned that war has no redeeming value. Survival is what counts most, not conquest. When a man fears being sent to the front lines, Frederic tells him a solid bump on the head will send him to an infirmary instead. His later shooting of the engineer for refusing to help push the truck does not represent a heightened sense of mission, however. In fact, it means just the opposite—the respect Frederic had for human life at the beginning of the novel has been replaced by the obscenity of duty. Shooting a soldier who refuses to obey an order comes as easily to him as getting blown up by a mortar shell, because neither requires thought, only reaction. Is something more than the will to live necessary to retain a sense of humanity, one beyond the acceptance of force as a way to resolve conflict? Dr. Rinaldi finds his answer to this question in the comfort brought by drink and promiscuity. The priest from Abruzzi finds solace in comforting others. And Frederic finds joy in the beauty of a life lived in love, at least for a while.

Catherine Barkley, a recreation of Agnes von Kurowsky, is the nurse who cares for Frederic while he recuperates from his leg wound in a Milan hospital. He doesn't mean what he says the first time he tells her he loves her. He's then surprised to learn that she doesn't mean it either. The thought that love can be a game for someone beside himself never enters his head. Frederic concludes that she may be a little crazy.

When sent to the front lines, however, he discovers that he misses Catherine—and he's pleased to find her assigned to his care after he is wounded. She must have been pleased to see him as well, because the two fall far enough in love to overcome their war-wrought cynicism. They don't fall so deeply, however, as to prevent Frederic from responding negatively to the news that Catherine is going to have a baby. He sees the impending birth as an inconvenience, and there's no indication that anything happened during the couple's idyllic winter in Switzerland to make him change his mind. When the baby is born dead, he shows no emotion whatsoever. He doesn't seem particularly broken up by Catherine's dying of a hemorrhage, either.

Is he in shock? Does his sense of loss run too deep for words? Has he retreated to that place in his heart where the war has eradicated his compassion for others? Or is he bitter from losing Catherine, the same way Hemingway was when Agnes von Kurowsky left him for an officer in the Italian army? Could it be that Hemingway isn't so much exacting his revenge on Agnes as he is symbolically killing off his divorced wife, Hadley, and their only child as a sign of loyalty and devotion to his second wife, Pauline, and their newly born Patrick?

Actress Jennifer Jones as Catherine Barkley in a scene from the 1957 film version of Hemingway's *A Farewell To Arms*.

Catherine Barkley

Like Agnes von Kurowsky, Catherine Barkley is free-spirited, independent-minded, and beautiful. As Agnes did with Ernest, she volunteers to work nights so she can be with Frederic as he recuperates. Catherine also shares traits with Brett in *The Sun Also Rises*, as well as Hemingway's model for Brett, Duff Twysden. All three women have in some way lost beloved men in the war, and prefer to play at the game of love rather than participate in the kinds of more meaningful relationships they no longer believe in.

Catherine's attitude changes abruptly, however, when she and Frederic fall in love. She now behaves more like a one-dimensional combination of Hemingway's submissive, eager-to-please first wife, Hadley, and his adoring, self-sacrificing second wife, Pauline. Catherine is so thoroughly committed to Frederic's happiness, she worries he will feel trapped when she tells him she is expecting a baby. She even goes so far as to announce her intention to bear alone the burden of raising their child—a responsibility both Hadley and Pauline shouldered to an extent with their children by Hemingway.

In the novel, Frederic's child is stillborn, and we as readers will never know what kind of a relationship they might have had. We can infer what Frederic's level of commitment might have been, however, by examining Hemingway's behavior toward his own children. Immediately after Patrick's birth in June of 1928, he left Pauline and the newborn for a six-week writing and fishing trip to Wyoming. That December, while Ernest was traveling to Florida with his son Bumby, he received a telegram that his father had died. When their train stopped in Baltimore, Ernest paid a conductor $40 to make sure Bumby arrived safely in Florida and headed, alone, for Chicago. (It didn't bother the five-year-old boy. He'd just gotten off a ship in New York after crossing the Atlantic without either parent.)

Frederic shows no emotion when the baby is stillborn—and neither does Catherine. Her last words are of concern for Frederic. Nothing she says, however, can inspire a response much greater than the **stoicism** he exhibited during his time on the front lines. War and love, Hemingway seems to be telling us, amount to the same thing in the end: pain and loss.

In this sense, Catherine proves the more heroic of Hemingway's two main characters. She displays the courage needed to risk the pain that might come from falling in love with another soldier soon after her fiancé's death. She doesn't hesitate to resolve the issue of her pregnancy alone if Frederic feels their child will be a burden he doesn't want to bear. She uncomplainingly suffers whatever hardships the war inflicts upon them. Nowhere, however, is the difference in courage between the two lovers more apparent than on Catherine's deathbed. Almost all her last words are intended to make her lover feel better. Death is nothing more than "a dirty trick," she tells him. Frederic, of course, only thinks about how her death will effect his life.

Frederic, like Jake Barnes of *The Sun Also Rises*, is more anti-heroic than heroic. But Jake elicits more sympathy. Trying to find meaning in his world, he seems more real, more human. Frederic, on the other hand, adheres to no philosophy, follows no vision, gives no reason for being in the war, and reveals little concern for anyone but himself. With Catherine, he experiences what it feels like to be loved, but is incapable of following her example. The best he can do is narrate a story that honors her memory.

Major Theme

Manhood

World War I caused many people to question the values they had inherited from the past—the ones that had failed to prevent the catastrophe of more than twenty million deaths—and search for a new system of concepts that could withstand the worst of what humankind was capable of. The characters in *The Sun Also Rises* and *A Farewell to Arms* provide Hemingway's response to his search for a new definition of manhood. Hemingway's concept of what it means to be a real man is clearly defined by the secondary characters against whom his main characters, Jake Barnes and Frederic Henry, are measured.

The starting point for Hemingway's definition of manhood is death. Since death ends all activity, including thought, there

Hemingway traveled with U.S. troops in Europe as a World War II correspondent in 1944.

is no afterlife. If there is any reward for living, it is in the immediate gratification of sensual pleasures. This is one of the reasons why the characters Hemingway admires consume so much alcohol. They enjoy it. They never get drunk, however. No matter how much wine Dr. Rinaldi consumes in *A Farewell to Arms*, he always manages to control his behavior. Mike Campbell of *The Sun Also Rises*, by contrast, is rarely in control when he drinks and often makes a fool of himself.

Rinaldi also engages in frequent sexual activity, but unlike Brett Ashley of *The Sun Also Rises*, his escapades don't end in frustration. They provide pleasure enjoyed for its own sake. Similarly, the doctor's contracting syphilis is not a punishment for sin—a pre–World War I concept—but the natural consequence of living life to its fullest.

Because life is pleasurable and death is nothing, mortality is something to be avoided. What separates the Hemingway man from those who try not to put themselves in situations where their lives might be threatened, however, is not a fear of death. It's a willingness to confront the enemy of life all the while knowing that any triumph is only temporary. The Hemingway man may be afraid of dying, but he cannot give in to the fear. He can't even show it. This is one of the reasons why Hemingway places his characters in bullfighting arenas and the front lines of war. He's providing us with role models of how real men act in the direct presence of death: with "grace under pressure."

A combination of courage and discipline, "grace under pressure" is the only acceptable way for real men to respond when confronting their own mortality. Anything less is cowardly. Each confrontation with death, then, is a test of manhood. For those who pass this test, life is sweeter. To appreciate the true value and full feeling of being alive, then, requires the intensity of emotion that comes with continual struggles against death.

Frederic Henry is not this kind of man. His wound from the war is accidental, and in several subsequent opportunities to confront death, he runs. He runs from the war, he runs from Italy, and he runs to God when he sits by Catherine on her deathbed. Ironically, it is the dying Catherine who comes closer to exemplifying the Hemingway ideal of "grace under pressure." She consistently shows more concern for Frederic's well-being than her own impending doom.

Hemingway uses other characters as well to illustrate his definition of manhood. The surgeon Dr. Valentini performs an operation on Frederic's leg when a team of less daring doctors want to wait six months, and the ambulance driver Bonello efficiently shoots in the head the sergeant Frederic has only wounded for refusing to obey his order. Valentini and Bonello aren't in danger of dying, but they exhibit the kind of self-assurance that comes with having passed tests of manhood. The same can be said of Rinaldi, who is contrasted with the sensitive, seemingly unmanly priest from Abruzzi. At the beginning of the novel, Rinaldi claims to be in love with Catherine Barkley, but he quickly gives her up to Frederic rather than become involved in a complicated relationship with them both. Pedro Romero, Hemingway's masculinist hero from *The Sun Also Rises*, responds in a similar way when Brett Ashley wants to end their relationship. He heads for the door.

Hemingway also headed for the door in his relationships with women, but his exits were not characterized by the kinds of swaggering independence displayed by Rinaldi and Romero. After being dumped by Agnes von Kurowsky, he never left a lover or a wife without having secured the affection of the next woman to whom he was attracted. If the attraction wasn't reciprocated to the degree he needed, he stayed put. During five of the twelve years he was married to Pauline Pfeiffer, he carried on an affair with the beautiful Jane Mason. If she hadn't been unwilling to leave her wealthy husband and two children, she might very well have become the third Mrs. Hemingway.

One final note: Real men don't talk. They're silent as well as strong. The qualities possessed by real men don't need to be discussed because they are innate. They cannot be learned; only lived. You are either a man of action, like the kind Hemingway admires, or you're not a real man. There's no in-between.

When a character Hemingway admires doesn't want to talk about something, it is usually some act of heroism he performed. Talking about an action reduces its value. Hemingway wasn't often able to meet this standard. He not only talked about the heroic acts he performed, he elaborated on them so often he came to believe these exaggerations were true. Had he been true to his code, Hemingway might have aged into a more mature version of his masculine ideal—someone like the truly self-confident Count Mippipopolous in *The Sun Also Rises*, or the empirically wise Count Greffi in *A Farewell to Arms*. As it turned out, older versions of Jake Barnes and Frederic Henry seem to be the best he could do.

Photographer Robert Capa (far left), with Ernest Hemingway (far right) during a wartime assignment.

Major Symbol

Rain

Rain is a timeworn device that writers have used for centuries
to reflect the emotions of the characters they are writing about.
Happy times are reflected by good weather, sad times are
accompanied by bad: think of it as a literary faucet. Frederic and
Catherine enjoy a beautiful summer of romance, but one night
it rains, and Catherine dreams of seeing herself or Frederic
dead. The night Frederic leaves for the front, it rains. It rains
through most of the Italian retreat from Caporetto, it rains
when the bartender in Stresa warns Frederic that he is about
to be arrested for desertion, and it rains on and off as the lovers
row to the safety of neutral Switzerland. Rain in the form of
snow provides some relief as Frederic and Catherine settle
down for the winter in a cabin near Montreux, but the deserter
who's made his "separate peace" with the war knows all along
that if life cannot break you, it will kill you.

This is exactly what happens. Frederic and Catherine move
in the spring to have their baby in a hospital, but the baby is
born dead, Catherine dies shortly afterwards from an unstop-
pable hemorrhage, and Frederic walks back to their hotel in the
rain. What's ironic is that it really did rain in all the instances
Hemingway wrote about. He purposely synchronized Frederic
and Catherine's movements with the historical timetable, rather
than make up a weather pattern to coincide with his story.

Timeline

1899 Ernest Miller Hemingway is born on July 21 in Oak Park, Illinois, to Clarence Edmunds Hemingway and Grace Hall Hemingway.

1914 World War I begins after Archduke Franz Ferdinand of Austria-Hungary is assassinated in Serbia.

1915 German submarine sinks the ocean liner *Lusitania* with American citizens on board.

1917 America enters World War I on the side of the Allies. Hemingway graduates from Oak Park High School.

1918 Hemingway is wounded by a mortar shell on July 8 while on duty with the Red Cross in Italy. He falls in love with Nurse Agnes von Kurowsky.

1919 World War I ends in January. Hemingway sails home the same month. Agnes sends a letter in March breaking off their engagement. The Senate limits U.S. participation in League of Nations and refuses to ratify Treaty of Versailles that ends World War I.

1920 The Eighteenth Amendment prohibits manufacture, sale, and transportation of alcohol. The Nineteenth Amendment gives women the right to vote. Hemingway moves to Chicago, where he falls in love with Hadley Richardson.

1921 Ernest and Hadley marry in September, and sail on December 8 for Paris.

1922 The couple lives off Hadley's inheritance and Hemingway's assignments from the *Toronto Star*. He covers the Greco-Turkish War.

1923 Hemingway visits Spain and sees his first bullfight. *Three Stories and Ten Poems*, his first book, is published in Paris. Hadley gives birth in Toronto to their only child, John Hadley Nicanor, on October 10.

1924 Hemingway works as an editor on Ford Maddox Ford's *transatlantic review*.

1925 Hemingway meets Pauline Pfeiffer. He travels with friends to Spain where he gathers material for *The Sun Also Rises*. *In Our Time* is published in New York.

1926 *The Sun Also Rises* is published. Ernest and Hadley separate.

1927 Hemingway divorces Hadley, marries Pauline, and sees publication of the short story collection *Men Without Women*.

1928 Pauline gives birth to Patrick in Kansas City on June 28. Hemingway's father commits suicide on December 6.

Timeline

1929 Ernest and Pauline return to Paris. *A Farewell to Arms* is published one month before the Stock Market crashes and the Great Depression begins.

1930 Hemingways move to Key West, Florida. *A Farewell to Arms* sold to Hollywood.

1932 *Death in the Afternoon* is published to unfavorable reviews. Pauline gives birth to their second son, Gregory. Franklin Delano Roosevelt introduces social security, welfare, and unemployment insurance.

1933 Hemingway's third collection of short stories, *Winner Take Nothing*, is published to unfavorable reviews. He begins writing for *Esquire*. He goes hunting big game on his first African safari. Adolf Hitler's National Socialist Party comes to power in Germany. The Eighteenth Amendment is repealed.

1934 Stricken with dysentery, Hemingway is flown past Mount Kilimanjaro to a hospital in Nairobi. The mountain is later featured in "Snows of Kilimanjaro."

1935 *Green Hills of Africa* is published.

1936 "Snows of Kilimanjaro" is published in *Esquire*. "The Short Happy Life of Francis Macomber" is published in *Cosmopolitan*. Hemingway meets journalist Martha Gelhorn, who is eighteen years his junior.

1937 Hemingway covers the Spanish Civil War for the American Newspaper Alliance. *To Have and Have Not* is published. He writes his only full-length play, *The Fifth Column*.

1938 *The Fifth Column* and the *First Forty-Nine Stories* is published. Hemingway writes anti-fascist articles for the left-wing magazine *Ken* and short stories about Spanish Civil War.

1939 Hemingway lives with Martha Gelhorn in Cuba. He ends his marriage to Pauline. World War II begins in Europe.

1940 *The Fifth Column* opens on Broadway. *For Whom the Bell Tolls* is published. Hemingway divorces Pauline Pfeiffer, and marries Martha Gelhorn.

1941 Martha, accompanied by Ernest, covers war between Japan and China. Together, they interview Chiang Kai-shek. The Japanese attack Pearl Harbor.

1942 Hemingway settles at Finca Vigia villa in Cuba, and searches for German submarines in his fishing boat *Pilar*. President Roosevelt orders the internment of Japanese Americans in concentration camps.

1944 Hemingway departs to serve as Collier's war correspondent with the Royal Air Force. He accompanies an infantry regiment across Normandy.

Timeline

1945   Hemingway divorces Martha Gelhorn. German forces surrender in the spring, followed by Japanese in August after the atomic bombing of Hiroshima and Nagasaki. The Cold War begins.

1946   Hemingway marries Mary Walsh.

1947   Hemingway is awarded the Bronze Star for meritorious service as a war correspondent. He works on *Garden of Eden*.

1948   Hemingway is interviewed for biographical pieces by *Life* and *Cosmopolitan*. The State of Israel is founded in Palestine. Apartheid is established in South Africa.

1950   *Across the River and Into the Trees* is published to disastrous reviews. Mood swings, always a part of Hemingway's personality, become wider-ranging and more pronounced.

1951   Hemingway's mother Grace dies. His former wife Pauline dies from a tumor at the age of fifty-six. He works on *Islands in the Stream*, which would be published posthumously in 1970.

1952   *Life* publishes *The Old Man and the Sea*, an expanded chapter from *Islands in the Stream*, in a single issue. Five million copies sell in two days.

1953 Hemingway wins the Pulitzer Prize for *The Old Man and the Sea*.

1954 Hemingway suffers severe injuries from two plane crashes in two successive days in Kenya and Uganda. He is awarded Nobel Prize for Literature.

1955 Hemingway works on the film version of *The Old Man and the Sea*, and comes down with nephritis and hepatitis from the trip to Africa.

1957 Hemingway begins reviewing sketches made thirty-five years earlier in Paris, which will become *A Moveable Feast*.

1960 Hemingway checks into the Mayo Clinic for depression. He is given electroshock therapy. Woolworth lunch counter sit-ins in Greensboro, North Carolina, launch the Civil Rights Movement.

1961 Hemingway is unable to contribute a few lines to a presentation volume for President John F. Kennedy. He can no longer put words on paper. He is taken back to the Mayo Clinic after three suicide attempts for more electroshock therapy. He loses his short-term memory. Hemingway convinces his doctors he is well, returns to Ketchum, and commits suicide on July 2.

Hemingway's Most Important Works

"Soldier's Home" (1925)

The Sun Also Rises (1926)

"Hills Like White Elephants" (1927)

A Farewell to Arms (1929)

"A Clean Well-Lighted Place" (1933)

"The Snows of Kilimanjaro" (1936)

"The Short Happy Life of Francis Macomber" (1938)

For Whom the Bell Tolls (1940)

The Old Man and the Sea (1952)

A Moveable Feast (1964)

Glossary

aficionado
One who possesses a deeper understanding of a subject or event.

dehumanization
Any process which deprives or negates the qualities or attributes that make a person human.

Eighteenth Amendment
Prohibited the manufacture, sale, and transportation of alcohol in the United States from 1917 until the amendment was repealed in 1933.

escapist
Any means of avoiding an unpleasant situation.

fiesta
A celebration of a religious holiday or a festive party.

impotence
Lacking power or ability.

matador
The principal bullfighter in a bullfight who guides the bull with a *muleta*, or red cloth, and then, in many countries, kills it with a sword thrust.

Glossary

modernism
A style in the humanities that rejects traditionally accepted forms of expression and emphasizes individual experimentation.

nationalist
Someone who advocates or fights for his or her country's independence or dominance.

nihilistic
Expressing extreme skepticism of any values or moral judgments.

shrapnel
Fragments from an exploding or exploded shell.

stoicism
Showing no response to any emotion. Submitting without complaint to the inevitable or unavoidable necessity.

tour de force
Exceptional achievement using skill, intelligence, and other personal resources.

trench warfare
Combat in which each side occupies a system of protective trenches.

Sources

Information about Ernest Hemingway's life comes primarily
from Jeffrey Meyers' *Hemingway: A Biography* (New York,
NY: Harper & Row, 1985) and Carlos Baker's *Ernest
Hemingway: A Life Story* (New York, NY: Charles Scribner's
Sons, 1969).

Further information about Hemingway's life and the time he
spent in Paris after World War I, in Spain during the
Spanish Civil War, and in France during World War II comes
primarily from A.E. Hotchner's *Hemingway and His World*
(New York, NY: Vendome Books, 1989). Meyers, Baker, and
Hotchner are the most noted of all Hemingway scholars.

The five weeks Hemingway spent in combat and the making
of *A Farewell to Arms* are carefully reconstructed in Michael
Reynolds's *Hemingway's First War* (Princeton, NJ: Princeton
University Press, 1976).

Biographical information not covered in the above-mentioned
works comes from the fourth edition of Carlos Baker's
Hemingway: The Writer as Artist (Princeton, NJ: Princeton
University Press, 1972).

Air Marshall Sir Peter Wykeham's comment about Hemingway
being more concerned about proving he wasn't cowardly first
appeared in the article "Hair Raising" (*London Times*, August 5,
1969, p.8).

Further Information

Books

Charles River Editors. *American Legends: The Life of Ernest Hemingway*. Seattle, WA: CreateSpace Independent Publishing Platform, 2013.

Fitch, Noel R. *Walks In Hemingway's Paris: A Guide To Paris For The Literary Traveler*. New York, NY: St. Martin's Griffin, 1999.

Meyers, Jeffrey. *Hemingway: A Biography*. Boston, MA: Da Capo Press, 1999.

Reynolds, Michael. *Hemingway: The Paris Years*. New York, NY: W. W. Norton & Company, 1999.

Websites

www.hemingwayhome.com

www.biography.com/people/ernest-hemingway-9334498

www.nobelprize.org/nobel_prizes/literature/laureates/1954/
hemingway-bio.html

www.jfklibrary.org/Research/The-Ernest-Hemingway-Collection

www.hemingwaysociety.org

Bibliography

Baker, Carlos. *Ernest Hemingway: A Life Story*. New York, NY: Charles Scribner's Sons, 1969.

Baker, Carlos. *Hemingway: The Writer as Artist*. Princeton, NJ: Princeton University Press, 1952.

Baker, Sheridan. *Ernest Hemingway: An Introduction and Interpretation*. New York, NY: Holt, Rinehart and Winston, 1967.

Burgess, Anthony. *Ernest Hemingway and His World*. New York, NY: Charles Scribner's Sons, 1978.

Gurko, Leo. *Ernest Hemingway and the Pursuit of Heroism*. New York, NY: Thomas Y. Crowell, 1968.

Hays, Peter L. *Ernest Hemingway*. New York, NY: Continuum, 1990.

Hemingway, Ernest. *A Farewell to Arms*. New York, NY: Charles Scribner's Sons, 1929.

Hemingway, Ernest. *The Complete Short Stories*. Charles Scribner's Sons, 1987.

Hemingway, Ernest. *The Sun Also Rises*. Charles Scribner's Sons, 1926.

Hotchner, A.E. *Papa Hemingway: A Personal Memoir*. New York, NY: Random House, 1966.

Hotchner, A.E. *Hemingway and His World*. New York, NY: The Vendome Press, 1989.

Kipling, Rudyard. *The Kipling Sampler*. New York, NY: Fawcett, 1957.

Meyers, Jeffrey. *Hemingway: A Biography*. New York, NY: Harper & Row, 1985.

Owen, Wilfred. "Dulce et Decorum Est." *Chief Modern Poets of Britain and America, Vol I: Fifth Edition*. New York, NY: Macmillan, 1970.

Reynolds, Michael. *Hemingway's First War*. Princeton, NJ: Princeton University Press, 1976.

Waldhorn, Arthur. *A Reader's Guide to Ernest Hemingway*. New York, NY: Farrar, Straus, Giroux, 1972.

Wykeham, Sir Peter. "Hair Raising," *Times* (London: August 5, 1969), p.8. Quoted by Jeffrey Meyers in *Hemingway: A Biography*. New York, NY: Harper & Row, 1985, pp. 406-407.

Index

About the Author

Richard Andersen, PhD, teaches writing and literature at Springfield College in Massachusetts. His twenty-nine published books include novels, literary criticism, books on writing, a biography, and an examination of contemporary education. A former Fulbright Professor in Norway, Karolyi Foundation Fellow in France, and James Thurber Writer in Residence at Ohio State University, he won his college's Excellence in Teaching Award and was also nominated by his college for the Carnegie Foundation's United States Professor of the Year Award. For Cavendish Square, he has written *Abraham Rodriguez* and *Walter Dean Meyers*.